Anyone who spends a few minutes with Andy and Joan can't help but catch something—like vision, energy, enthusiasm, and missionary zeal!

—**Joni Eareckson Tada**, president, Joni and Friends Ministries and author of *Holiness in Hidden Places*

❦

Joan and Andy Horner represent the highest levels of integrity. They have become leaders in our industry and have done it the right way.

—**Neil Offen**, President, Direct Selling Association

❦

Andy Horner spent seventeen years at Home Interiors and he affected us. Although he moved on, that did not erase the imprint he made; it's still there and we're better off for it.

—**Donald J. Carter**, former CEO and Chairman of the Board, Home Interiors and Gifts

❦

The launching of Premier Designs through Andy and Joan Horner was verily and truly a providence of God. In the devoted and dedicated people who work for the company, and in the many recipients of the goodness and kindness of the organization, a whole generation has been marvelously blessed.

—**W. A. Criswell**, Pastor Emeritus, First Baptist Church, Dallas Church, Dallas

❦

In a world that is crying for caring, Andy and Joan heard. Their awesome creation, Premier Designs, reflects and supports the much deeper beauty of two lives dedicated to God's designs of spreading His truth in the ministry of healing—spiritually, emotionally, and physically.
—**Dr. Hazel Goddard**, founder of Christian Counseling Ministries

꙳

If Andy and Joan were described to me without having met them, I don't think I could believe they were real people. Real? Are they ever! Real Christians. Real workers. Real examples. Their love for the Lyons family has been an immeasurable blessing. Their involvement in our Chicago inner city ministry has been an incredible encouragement. Real friends. Real servants.
—**Pastor Charles Lyons**, Armitage Baptist Church, Chicago

꙳

BY CHANCE OR BY DESIGN?

By Chance or By Design?

The Story of Premier Designs and Founders, Andy and Joan Horner

Andrew J. Horner
with Andrea Horner, Ph.D.
and Dave Wyrtzen, Th.D.

Premier Designs INC.

Scripture quotations marked TLB are taken from *The Living Bible*, © 1971 by Tyndale House Publishers, Inc., Wheaton, Illinois 60189. Used by permission. All rights reserved.

Scripture quotations marked NLT are taken from the *Holy Bible, New Living Translation*, © 1996 by Tyndale House Publishers, Inc., Wheaton, Illinois 60189. Used by permission. All rights reserved.

Scripture quotations marked NIV are taken from the HOLY BIBLE, NEW INTERNATIONAL VERSION®, "NIV"© 1973, 1978, 1984 International Bible Society. Used by permission of Zondervan Publishing House. All rights reserved. The "NIV" and "New International Version"® trademarks are registered in the United States Patent and Trademark Office by International Bible Society. Use of either trademark requires permission of International Bible Society.

Scripture quotations marked KJV are taken from the *Holy Bible, King James Version*.

Cover design by Leonard Fisher

Library of Congress Cataloging-in-Publication Data

Horner, Andy, 1924–
    By chance or by design?: The story of Premier Designs, Inc. and founders, Andy & Joan Horner / by Andy Horner with Andrea Horner and Dave Wyrtzen.
        p.cm.

    1. Premier Designs.   2. Horner, Andy, 1924–   3. Horner, Joan.   4. Jewelry trade—United States.   5. Businesspeople—United States-Biography.   6. New business enterprises—United States—Case studies.   1. Horner, Andrea.   11. Wyrtzen, David, 1949–   111. Title.
HD9747.U54P734 2000
338.7'6882'092-dc21
[B]

                                                                                    99-050223

04   03   02   01   00

10   9   8   7   6   5   4   3   2   1

❧

This book is dedicated with much
gratitude to all who have helped build
Premier in this first generation.

❧

Contents

PART THREE: THE PROOF OF PREMIER

Preface to the Second Edition

We have learned much since Premier Designs began in 1985, and many things have changed since the first printing of this book in 1995. People have come and gone. Systems have developed and expanded. But our foundational principles remain the same.

One of the main things we have discovered is that you can build a successful business, and more importantly a fulfilling life, on biblical principles. We have a *philosophy* that believes in God, a *purpose* that enriches lives, and a *plan* that will take us into millions of homes with hope in our heart. Premier Designs is not a religion, denomination, or missionary organization. It is a well-managed and successful corporation that wants to honor God and serve people.

America is our homeland and we love it. However, our hearts are saddened by much that is happening in our country. People are full of fear and hopelessness. They need to see those who profess to be Christians stop preaching and start practicing what Christians believe. They need to see corporations more focused on a *top line* of people than on a *bottom line* of profit. They need to see corporations and companies that have character. Character involves integrity and truth. These are the ingredients that build trust. Trust is the glue that not only binds companies and employees but also will bring unity to the people of America.

May those who read these pages see that life is more than by chance; it is by design. We cannot fail when "in God we trust."

Andy Horner
January 2000

Preface to the First Edition

*H*ave you ever sat down and reflected on the past? Who you are? What has happened to you? Why it happened? I never had until we started to put this book together. As I looked back on my life, I could see the turning points, the important choices that were made by me and by others, as well as the events that seemed insignificant at the time but turned out to be so important. I wish I had known as I was going through these times that all the struggles, the disappointments, and the heartaches were part of a plan meant to help me discover real success and fulfillment. This is the story of how Premier Designs came about, the company that became the culmination of my life experiences—not by chance, but by design.

Although Premier Designs developed out of life experience and the heart, it is not a company that ignores good business practices or common sense. It is a heavenly-focused company with an earthly application, built on two basic principles: *To Honor God and Serve People.*

Is it perfect? No. Are there mistakes and problems? Yes. But I can honestly say that most of my mistakes have resulted from running the business from my heart. A business run from the heart means that sometimes people and their needs come before the practical or efficient thing to do. People are the most important asset. Whatever we can do for them will ultimately be good for Premier Designs.

Andy Horner
1995

Acknowledgments

*M*any of the ideas in this book are not original, but have come from those who have had a great impact on my life. I thank all who have shared with me and taught me, especially:

My mother, *Sarah Smyth Horner*, an Irish scrub lady who gave birth to sixteen children, who had no education but was so wise. She instilled in me the qualities of hard work and persistence. She prayed for me, disciplined me, loved me, and always demanded my best.

Lorne Lynch, owner of Lynch's Meat Market, who taught me when I was a young lad the value of hard work; *Jay Lansford*, my first manager at Johnson Wax, who was hard to please but taught me much; *Dr. William Smith*, of Xerox, who convinced me that I had strengths, but also weaknesses; and *Mary Crowley*, founder of Home Interiors, who taught me so much, but nothing more important than "you build the people and they will build your business." She reminded me that you cannot outgive God and taught me to not look at people as they appear, but to see in them what they can become. A woman of true integrity, she practiced what she preached.

How can I express my gratitude to *Joan*, my wife of over fifty years? Her encouragement, love, patience, and help have changed my life. Her desire to do what is right and in the right way keeps me on the right track. It is true that behind every successful man is a dedicated, supportive woman. To my five grown children, *Andrea, Sarah, Tim, Mary,* and *Tommy,* all gifts from God, who had to eat and so kept me motivated. When I might have quit, they were the reason I did not.

Thanks to *Leonard Fisher*, Premier's Art Director, for the art work. And to *all the Premier Associates and Jewelers* who helped out—big thank you.

Special thanks to *Andrea Horner*, my daughter, who researched and wrote most of this story, and *Dave Wyrtzen*, my counselor and friend, who helped Andrea try to fit seventy years into these pages. They know me well and have presented the story as it was and is.

My prayer is that this book may honor the Lord whom I serve and be a blessing to those who are kind enough to read its pages.

Introduction

*S*uccess in the Internet generation is about mastering new technology. Computerized telephone answering services, voice mail, faxes, spread sheets, and e-mail—these are the tools needed to achieve a prosperous bottom line in the communication age.

My name is Michael. As a graduate of a prestigious university with a degree in business, I thought I knew what it takes to build a successful company in a technological world. Then my wife Linda met a friend who was involved in selling jewelry. They had met for lunch, and Linda noticed the exquisite earrings that set off her friend's stylish outfit. "Mary, where did you get those earrings, and where did you get the money to dress like that?" she asked.

Mary laughed. "They're not all that expensive and if you'll come to Barbara's house tomorrow night, I'll show you a lot more than these earrings."

Linda went to the show and did come home with a lot more than jewelry. "Michael, look at what I bought!" She modeled her evening purchases—Czarina necklace, Violetta pin, and Illusion earrings. Even the names sounded rich and exotic, and I responded with the required *oohs* and *ahs*. Then she dropped the bomb. "Michael, this is terrific stuff, and we can sell it!"

Sell it? The last thing I wanted was for my wife to get involved in some direct sales jewelry company. But Linda continued, "I want to start my own business like Mary. This Premier Designs company offers an incredible opportunity. Look at this marketing plan."

Just what I needed—my wife involved in some get rich quick, multi-level pyramid scheme. But I did look at the plan, and instead of high-sounding promises, there was the authentic ring of down-home values, good old American hard work, and basic common sense. When Mary made over four hundred dollars at her first home show, it seemed it wouldn't hurt for her to go ahead. She would soon burn out, and it would be time for her to try to find herself in some other crazy dream.

Rather than burning out, however, she became more excited, her confidence soared, and her business grew steadily. I found myself caring for our kids a couple of nights a week, especially as Linda's home show schedule accelerated before the Christmas holidays. After New Year's things would settle down and our home could return to normal, I thought. Or would it?

"Michael, I've won an achievement award!" Linda told me excitedly. "I want you to come to the January rally with me. It will be good for us. We can meet new friends. I can get new ideas for developing my business, and you can evaluate Premier Designs for yourself." So we sent in our registrations, and I found myself checking into the Dallas Hyatt Regency.

How do you describe a Premier Designs rally? It's a combination of business training seminar, old-fashioned revival and camp meeting, pep rally, and warm family reunion. It's a cross between a Billy Graham crusade and a *Jeopardy* show. Linda and I found ourselves deep in the heart of Texas hustling from seminars on "Managing Your Money" to training sessions covering bookings, home shows, and managing your time and your business. I've never hugged so many people, seen so many smiles, and felt such honest concern.

There was no hype about how you could be driving a brand new Cadillac and vacationing in Cancun if you simply signed on. Instead, I heard testimonies of single mothers who found friends, a support system, and a way to meet their financial needs and be with their kids. Former contractors and engineers shared how they survived seismic shifts in their industry, paid off their debts, and found fulfillment by building into the lives of others when they found Premier. These people talked not about "direct sales" but about "direct service." They talked about "enriching every life they touched," "remembering that people are more important than profits," and that "every individual is worthy and valuable, not because of what they do, but because God created them in His own image."

Was all this too good to be true? Could these traditional values of honesty, caring, and giving provide a foundation for a company that would be successful as we move into the twenty-first century? Modern companies talk about aggressive attack, hostile takeovers, and warlike competition. How could there be room in American business for a company that functions more like a nostalgic rerun of *The Waltons* than the latest *Die Hard* movie? A company that has integrity and tells the truth? A company that emphasizes that building a successful life is more important than building a successful business?

The growth of Premier Designs provided the objective proof I needed. Who could argue with the numbers? Premier is successful—through solid home office management, controlled growth in sales, skilled personnel, exquisite products, and careful planning for the future. The most hardened cynic could not argue with this.

But statistics do not answer deeper issues of credibility and trust. I received my answer to these questions on the Saturday morning of the rally as Andy Horner, the founder of Premier, shared from his heart.

As the orchestra and chorus came to the crescendo of their "Tribute to America," patriotism moistened everyone's eyes. Andy's heart for his adopted homeland was evident as he spoke. Where else on earth could the son of an alcoholic father, born into the hate and violence of Belfast, end up the cofounder and president of a successful company dedicated to honoring God and serving others? A stool was set center stage and Andy casually sat down. It was time to deliver his annual founder's address, entitled "Lest We Forget." He told more than the story of his life, but the story of Premier Designs.

This company and the truths it demonstrates have changed my life. It could change yours. It has given me renewed hope. Yes, this former no-nonsense business cynic with his spreadsheets and fax machines has recognized the revolutionary power of personal serving, caring, and giving even in the jungle of American business. It is no longer Linda's business; it is our business. The following pages explain why.

PART ONE

The Road to Premier

"Adventures always have risks, but they also have rewards. Don't let the past, good or bad, affect your present or determine your future."

ANDY HORNER

✺

"The things about my mother that I resented as a boy are the things that I am most grateful for as a man."

ANDY HORNER

✺

CHAPTER ONE

Irish Roots

*J*oan and I incorporated Premier Designs in Dallas, Texas, in November, 1985, but the beginnings of Premier can really be traced all the way back to Ireland in the 1920s. It's been a long road with many hills and valleys. Has it been easy? No. And for most of my years I was unaware of my final destination.

Last in Line

I was born at 3 Upper Charleville Street in Belfast on August 5, 1924, to Sarah Smyth and Andrew Horner. My mother worked in the linen factories as a weaver before her marriage, and part-time even after she had children. My father worked his entire life as a welder at the famous Belfast shipyards. Six days a week, he left for work in the dark each morning and came home after dark each night.

It was a difficult life. We had enough to eat, but barely, and wore hand-me-down clothes a size too big. There were enough coins to buy gas for the light and peat for the fire, but nothing extra. I can remember being excited to get an orange and some candy in my Christmas stocking.

I am sure that by 1924 my mother thought she was done having babies. The youngest of her twelve surviving children was seven years old. The tiny Irish row house had only a small living room and kitchen downstairs and two small bedrooms upstairs. The children slept four or five to a straw mattress and ate meals sitting on the stairs. When one of the kids left home, it was a big deal—it meant the next oldest got to graduate to the table. The household was already overflowing. Nonetheless, at age forty-four, my mother learned she was pregnant once again—with me.

I was born at home, delivered by my mother's sister. She and my mother were the neighborhood midwives. My brothers and sisters didn't exactly welcome me with open arms. I was one more mouth to feed and one more child to take care of. My mother said that I was her "angel pride from heaven sent," but the rest of the family thought I had been sent from somewhere else—and most of the time it felt like they wanted to send me back there.

Looking back on it, I can understand their feelings. Not only were we poor and living in a crowded house, but I cried constantly. Later we found out that I had been crying because of chronic ear infections and an abscessed eardrum. But at the time all the other children knew was that there was this fussy baby who made their lives even more difficult. As I grew older, their feeling that I was an afterthought and a bother remained the same. They did not hide the fact that they would rather not have me around. My mother made them play with me, and if they didn't, I told on them. Of course they considered me a tattletale pest and a tag-along. Whenever they could, they left me behind. If we played hide-and-seek, I would hide but they never came to find me. Even when I was older and we played cowboys and Indians, they would make me be the Indian, tie me to a tree, and leave me there. One day my brother Hughey got so disgusted with me that he threw me in a lake. I quickly learned how to swim!

Now I tell these stories as jokes, but they had an impact on me. I carried the feelings of rejection and being unwanted for many, many years—feelings forced even deeper inside by the pressure of growing up in a religiously divided country where I was taught to hate and fight. Only later in life did I learn that feelings can deceive us.

Belfast Battles

Ireland, an island the size of the state of Maine, is perched in the beautiful North Atlantic, surrounded by 1,700 miles of dramatic coastline. The Irish are friendly and hospitable, and among the most creative people on this earth. Ireland has produced more poets, playwrights, and American presidents than any other country of comparable size.

There is another side to Ireland, though. It is a place filled with hatred, bigotry, and violence. The people are proud and strong-willed. As a Protestant, I was brought up to hate and fear Catholics. Groups of Catholic toughs would cross the Crumlin Road—the division between the Protestant and Catholic neighborhoods—and harass us. They threw rocks and bottles, broke up our games, stole our balls, and taunted us. These battles weren't one-sided; we did our share of rock throwing as well. We felt vulnerable and learned at tender ages about hatred and intimidation.

In those days, the battles of my world carried over into our home. My dad was not around much. When he was, he had little to say. On payday, he joined his buddies at the pub and got drunk. When he got drunk, he got mean—almost every weekend was hell. I remember him roaring into our house many Saturday nights yelling, busting down doors, looking for a fight. Only my big brother Bill could control him. He would take Dad out of the house and walk him around until he sobered up. It was a hopeless life, both inside and outside our home, and when Bill emigrated to America in 1929, it got worse. Now there was no one to protect us from Catholic bullies and a drunken father.

Things became very desperate for our family. My mother loved Ireland and Charleville Street, her friends and family. But she wanted better for her children. Unbeknownst to my father, she made the biggest decision of her life—she decided to take me, my brother Hugh, and my sister Chrissie away from Ireland. Four of my brothers had already gone. Bill and Tommy were in America, and Sammy and Jim were in Canada. She wanted to take us to America, but health problems prevented this; so my brothers arranged for our passage to Canada.

The Duchess of Richmond

I still vividly remember the morning of April 8, 1931. A big, black car drove up in front of our house to drive us to the dock. I had never even seen a car before, let alone ridden in one, and I was excited. I raced around trying to hurry everyone up, running back and forth looking into the car. Finally, we all got in and drove off. I could hardly sit still. I squirmed from window to window trying to make sure that I didn't miss a thing. And then there she was, sitting in the Belfast harbor—*the Duchess of Richmond*, the big, beautiful ship that was going to take us to Canada. I didn't understand much about what we were doing or where we were going, but I was excited. I can remember walking on board and seeing the huge crystal chandeliers and the long tables loaded with food. I had never seen anything like this before, and certainly had never seen so much food. I couldn't wait for us to get going so I could start eating.

A group of friends from the Gospel Hall came to see us off. My mother had become a Christian before I was born, and she was a faithful member of the Machette Street Gospel Hall. Those Christian folks gathering around us to pray and sing just before we left is one of the sweetest memories I have of my childhood in Ireland. I can still hear them:

> God be with you till we meet again;
> By His counsels guide, uphold you,
> With His sheep securely fold you;
> God be with you till we meet again.

And then we were off. It was an act of faith, courage, and sacrifice for my fifty-one-year-old mother to leave her husband, family, friends, and beloved Ireland to give her youngest children opportunity and hope. Little did she know that the journey she began that day would lead, fifty-four years later, to the adventure of Premier Designs, a company that would touch thousands of lives in America and around the world with opportunity and hope. Was it the luck of the Irish? Just by chance? Or was there a greater design?

*"The legacy my mother left was not silver
or gold, but was worth so much more.
She taught me how to work hard and that
it was more blessed to give than to receive."*

Andy Horner

⚜

*"A sense of worth is not found in titles,
in possessions, or in who we know;
but is found in our relationship with God."*

Andy Horner

⚜

CHAPTER TWO

Woodstock Memories

After two weeks at sea, our ship arrived in St. John's, New Brunswick, and we boarded a train to Woodstock. It was a journey of over a thousand miles. All we had to eat was a can of cookies given as a going-away gift. When we arrived in the city of Woodstock, Ontario, there was no one there to meet us. I never did discover what caused the mix-up, but there we were, four Irish immigrants, standing on the train platform in a strange town in Canada. My mother did not wait long. There were only two cabs in town. She hailed one of them and asked the driver if he knew where Sam Horner lived. Surprisingly, he did. He drove us straight to 715 Dundas Street, above the Maple Dairy store. We climbed up eight flights of stairs and walked inside the flat where I was to live for the next fifteen years.

The Woodstock Paperboy

Compared to the fragments I remember of Ireland, my memories of Canada are full and vivid. The thing I remember most is work, work, work. At age seven, I started tossing papers. No matter what other activities or jobs

I had going, I met the 5:30 P.M. train from Toronto, rain or snow, six afternoons a week to get my papers to deliver. At the age of nine, I began working Saturdays at Lynch's Meat Market earning seventy-five cents a day; and at eleven, working summers and after school at the Maple Dairy, washing milk bottles, wrapping butter, and delivering orders. I sold produce (carrots and beans) door-to-door for five cents a bunch. I helped my mother scrub the floors and stairs in our building in exchange for free rent and ice. There were 120 steps and I remember every one. I calculated that I did this detested chore 520 times! We also cleaned apartments and offices night after night. Through it all, I kept throwing those newspapers.

Mother was from the old country culture that believed in hard work and no complaining. And my work never ended. Over and over again she made me do a job until I got it right. Talk about a hard taskmaster and a tough disciplinarian! I felt persecuted and picked on. She maintained strict standards and she expected me to meet them all. At the time I felt she was unfair and constantly punishing me, and I resented it. Now I cherish those values and work habits that she pounded into me. I can still hear her saying, "A job worth doing is worth doing right" and "Work as unto the Lord." Because of her legacy, I've never been afraid to work hard, and I never leave a job half done.

I also learned that "a penny saved is a penny earned." The poverty of Ireland and the hardships in Canada during the 1930s depression made frugality an absolute necessity for our family. Once after I had collected the money for my paper route, I dropped a dime in the snow on my way home. Mom made me go all the way back to where I had dropped it and dig around in the snow until I found it. Cold, humiliated, ashamed, I resented her making me scrounge around in the snow for one measly dime; but slowly I was learning the value of even one thin coin.

We ate day-old bread and cracked eggs. In fact, I thought all eggs came cracked. We never used more electricity or gas than absolutely necessary. We had to turn the lights off in every room as we left (a habit that continues to this day). At night we sat in the dark to cut down the light bill. Mother had few dresses, and we wore hand-me-downs that didn't fit. I had to tighten my belt to hold up pants that were too large. Mom made my pant cuffs inches deep so she could let them out as I grew. I hated being poor and felt embarrassed wearing those too-large castoffs, but I can still hear my mother say, "Son, you'll grow into them. It's what's on the inside that counts."

Liberal generosity is hardly expected from someone who works constantly just to pay the light bill, but my mother was one of the most generous people I ever knew. If you walked into her house and said you liked something, it was on your doorstep the next morning. People learned to be careful what they said about stuff in our house because it was easy to end up with something you didn't really like or want. Many times she gave away our food, clothing, and furniture. We would go without so someone else could have something they needed.

My mother's Bible is a precious treasure to me. It is in the Bible collection at Premier headquarters, and whenever I look through it, one thing always strikes me—it is filled with prayer cards and pledge cards for a number of missionaries. She told me that there was no greater thing we could do than help spread the gospel to all the world, and although she did not have much money, she gave generously. Her heart was with missions.

Mother gave more than her money, however; she gave herself. When she died in May of 1947, her funeral was one of the largest the city of Woodstock had ever seen. I was shocked. Hundreds of people came to pay their respects to this Irish scrub lady. We heard story after story of her many kindnesses. People I had never met told me how she had given them a gift of bread or soup, had nursed them and cared for their children, and had always had kind words of comfort, encouragement, and love. She left me a marvelous legacy of hard work and selfless giving.

The Woodstock Letterman

Yes, I worked hard, but that's not all I did as a boy. I entered the Chapel School at seven, the Princess School at ten, and the Woodstock Collegiate High School at thirteen. I was not what you would call a great student. Although I never failed a grade, I remained firmly planted near the bottom of my class. I preferred the social life. Visiting with my friends was a much higher priority than doing common, everyday homework. I was very talkative, liked being the center of attention, and couldn't sit still. I also had a short attention span and had difficulty focusing on one thing at a time. I tell people that I spent more time in the principal's office than in my classroom, which may be an Irishman's slight exaggeration, but not by much. Even though my mother's favorite expression was "children are to be seen and not heard," I was heard every time I was seen.

Because of my short attention span and my hands that sometimes shook, schools tested me regularly to figure out what was wrong with me. They tried pills to calm me down and help me concentrate, but nothing worked. I guess today they would diagnose me as hyperactive with attention deficit disorder, but back then they didn't have scientific labels for such things. They simply called me a pain in the neck.

Combine bad grades, bad behavior, and bad placement at the end of the line in a large family and you've got the ingredients for some low self-esteem. And then there were sports. I was a short, scrawny kid, too small to really be competitive, but I loved playing and had a strong desire to win. I had something to prove.

We had some athletic talent in my family. Bill, my older brother, played championship soccer in Ireland and professional soccer in the States. Despite the athletic genes passed down to the Horners, I had to overcome my size disadvantage by doing what I knew best—working at it harder than anyone else. I went to the YMCA and shot baskets hour after hour. Every spare minute, I was on the ice fine-tuning my hockey skills. I played catch and batted baseballs with anyone who would play with me. As a result, I played hockey and basketball all through high school, starring and lettering in both. In the summers I was one of the stars of city league baseball. My lack of achievement in the classroom is now legendary, and my musical career peaked when I performed my one instrumental solo, "Nearer My God to Thee," on my one dollar guitar. But athletics was the one place where my strong drive could generate success and I could get the recognition I craved. I had to be the best and I had to win. Sports became the way to do this because I sure wasn't that great in much else.

Sometimes I took this striving to achieve and needing to win too far. At one race at a school event, when I saw that I was not going to win, I simply pulled up and acted like I was hurt and unable to finish the race. If you can't win, I figured, then fake an injury. This approach also brought the added advantage of getting all that attention over my "injured leg."

Woodstock's "Mr. Personality"

As I look back, one thing that was evident during my growing-up years in Woodstock was my ability to relate to people. Whatever other struggles I had inside myself and in my life, I always liked people and could get along well with them. One example stands out in my mind. Thanks to the generosity of Jack Cole, one of our town's leaders, every summer I was able to go to Fisher's Glen, a YMCA camp. Two summers in a row I was elected "Best All Around Boy." This was quite an honor and I was one of the few boys who received it more than once. Natural leadership abilities were beginning to show up in my life—enthusiasm, a knack for understanding people, an outgoing personality, and an ability to get along with just about anyone. These traits have helped me overcome a lot and became important in my business success. I am grateful for the early opportunities through athletics and summer camp to develop these leadership characteristics.

Friends, awards at camp, and success in athletics were all a part of my childhood—but my dad wasn't. I never saw or heard from him after we left Ireland, and my memories of him are not positive. I saw other kids with their dads and imagined what it would be like to have a nice dad. I would go to the homes of my friends like Bob and Jimmy Davis and pretend that their families, especially their fathers, were mine. Their mom made us delicious donuts and their dad wrestled with us and helped us build things. I remember other dads who played ball with their sons and me, and who took me places and did things with me.

These men were kind and took an interest in me, but it wasn't the same as having a father of my own. A dad, a nice home, and a normal family life—that's what I longed for.

The Woodstock Decision

When we arrived in Woodstock, one of the first things my mother did was go to the nearby Gospel Hall to apply for membership. However, the Woodstock Brethren would not allow her to join their congregation because she didn't have the proper letter from her Brethren congregation in Ireland. They made us sit in the visitors' section at the back of the hall. With this reception, it didn't take us long to end up down the street at Oxford Street Baptist Church, a small congregation of one hundred people that became the center of our lives.

I know my mother's faith took on even deeper meaning for her in Canada than it had in Ireland. She missed Ireland and her friends and family. She was lonely and heartbroken, and I heard her crying many nights as she sat rocking in the dark. She sacrificed a great deal to bring us to Canada. Mom had a hard life. She was in poor health when we arrived in Woodstock and as the years went by, her health deteriorated further. She developed a serious problem with painful and debilitating varicose veins. She suffered every day but found hope and solace in the promises of the Bible. Her relationship with the Lord sustained her and gave her a peace and joy that can't be explained. "It is no vain thing to wait upon the Lord, son," she would say.

I am ashamed to admit it, but sometimes I thought she was nuts. I would come home and hear her talking in the kitchen and think we had company, only to go back there and see that she was talking to Jesus as if He were right there in the room. She read her Bible daily and claimed its promises with unquestioning faith. I saw her kneeling by her bed countless times and heard her singing as she worked. She sang hymns of heaven and of hope— hope that her suffering would end and that soon she would be in heaven with her Lord.

For years, my mother prayed that I too would become a Christian. When I was eleven, her prayers were answered. I accepted Jesus Christ as my Lord and Savior at a meeting at our little Baptist church. At around the same time, my brother Hugh became a Christian at an evangelistic tent meeting in Woodstock. Hugh felt called to be an evangelist, and I went with him as he preached on the street corners of Woodstock and nearby London. He also organized a "tract band" in Woodstock, and I helped him pass out gospel tracts all around the city. My mother was pleased that we were both working to bring others to the Lord. For her, there was nothing more impor- tant and worthwhile.

Our lives revolved around our church. For years, we walked the mile and a half to church almost every evening. We had young people's meetings on Monday, booster band on Tuesday, prayer meeting on Wednesday, choir practice on Thursday, church socials on Friday, prayer meeting on Saturday, and three services on Sunday. My mother seldom missed, and she made me go with her. But the older I got, the less I liked it. I got tired of going to church all the time. I had other things to do that I thought were more fun. I was getting fed up with her Bible read- ing and praying and hymn singing, and I was sick of her telling me what I could and couldn't do.

I rebelled. I ran away a couple of times, one time hitch- hiking almost twenty miles before I turned around and went back. I didn't go to church as much and started doing more things with friends who were not Christians. This worried and hurt my mother. I danced and played cards, things that my mother had taught me were sin. I stayed out late with my friends and tried to sneak in the house, and there she would be, sitting in the dark waiting for me. She disciplined me with the silent treatment. For days after one of these incidents she wouldn't speak to me, and I hated that too. I felt she wanted to control me and ruin my life.

The Woodstock Princess

When I was sixteen, we got a car, a 1934 Ford. Mother could no longer walk to our cleaning jobs, so she had to get a car in order to keep on working. I don't know where she got the money or what kind of deal she worked out for it, but she bought it. She wouldn't drive, so all the chauffeuring to and from jobs was left up to me. In the off hours, I got the car to myself.

All of a sudden I was the most popular guy in Woodstock. No one else my age had a car. Here I was, this poor kid from the East End, now running around with the rich kids from across the tracks. Although I had known these kids most of my life, we hadn't ever traveled in the same social circles. The town was socially segregated. The "East Enders" had the reputation of being poor, tough, and ready to fight. Our reputation was greatly exaggerated, but we played the role well. My gang was not known for our kindness and goodness, but we were known well by the Woodstock police. I became well acquainted with Chief Innis and the other six officers.

One of the well-to-do kids from the other side of town was Joan Taylor. Joan and I had both attended elementary school at the Princess School. I used to tease her a lot when we were growing up, and through our years of schooling she had no interest in me. She was smart and always ranked first or second in class. I ranked fortieth or forty-first, depending on whether my friend George was in class that day. I tried to cheat off her a few times, too, but she wouldn't let me. She was a good, moral girl who attended church regularly. She was also the prettiest girl in Woodstock, and way out of my league.

At the time I got my car and was expanding my social circles, Joan was dating a friend of mine named Bill. I asked out Joan's good friend, Shirley, so we could double date. I liked Shirley, and the four of us had some great times, but I also had another agenda. I was actually courting Joan, even though she didn't know it!

Joan and I got to know each other on these outings and became good friends. I loved it when she came and cheered me on at basketball games and baseball games even when my team, the East Enders, was playing Bill's team from St. Mary's. I thought she was just super even though she rooted for him, too. Of course, I was not going to move in on my friend, Bill, so I was just waiting for my opportunity to ask her out. Then came World War II.

When war broke out in Europe in 1939, three of my brothers joined the army and headed to England with the first Canadian division. Within the next couple of years, most of the able-bodied men in Woodstock enlisted to go fight the Germans. I was tired of school and tired of my mom and her expectations. I wanted to get away and have some adventure. So in 1941, at the age of seventeen, I joined the Royal Canadian Navy with the hope of seeing the world.

*"If a thing is worth doing,
it is worth doing well."*

SARAH HORNER, ANDY'S MOTHER

❧

*"It is sad, but true, that we sometimes
do not understand, nor appreciate fully,
the impact people have until they are dead."*

ANDY HORNER

❧

*"We can't control our past; but it's the
choices we make in the present, not what
happened in the past, that will determine
our success in the future."*

ANDY HORNER

❧

CHAPTER THREE

The Navy and Romance

Over the years I've told a lot of Navy stories. For example, the first time I went on board ship, I knew something was wrong when the command came to drop anchor, and when we did, the anchor sank straight to the bottom. There was no chain connecting it to the ship. I've often described myself as the Canadian Navy's number one torpedo chaser. We only had two torpedoes, so when we fired one and missed, I had to swim out to retrieve it so we could use it again. We sank a lot of ships—the problem was that most of them were our own. We were so lethal against ourselves that the Germans planned to commission us in their Navy. I've had some fun making up jokes about my Navy days, but in fact, those were deadly serious times.

The War in the North Sea

I went to signalman's school in Quebec for several months before I ever set foot on a ship. My first ship assignment was to an ammunitions barge on the run from Montreal to St. John's, Newfoundland, down the St. Lawrence River. This was disappointing because I had visions of being assigned to a sleek fighting destroyer. Finally, I was assigned to a convoy and sailed for the North Atlantic. My ship, the *Monnow*, was a frigate and our job was to sweep ahead for German U-boats. I was so nervous I couldn't even translate the first message that came in on my watch.

After this tour, we were reassigned to a British striking force. This involved trips through the Mediterranean, and later, a six-month tour on the "hell run" from Scotland, under the Arctic Circle, to the northern Russian port of Arch- angel. The Germans had conquered Norway by that time and were operating both U-boats and torpedo bombers in this corridor. The run lasted twenty-six days with unbearably long nights. Our ships were coated in ice. We were in total radio silence, with the Germans below us and above us—we were sitting ducks. All communication was by lights and flags, which kept Signalman Horner V58205 very busy.

These runs were pure hell. I watched ships sinking, water flaming, and bodies of the dead floating in the seas. I was scared, and every time our ship saw action, I rededicated my life to God and asked Him to protect me. Then, as soon as the threat was gone and we got into a safe port, I went right back to acting like He didn't exist and lived it up with the rest of the guys. I was sick and tired of all the God stuff from my upbringing, and I didn't want to think about it. But I also knew something was wrong. At night in my hammock I often tossed and turned uneasily. During my entire Navy experience I never had peace.

God's faithfulness amazes me. At that point in my life I ignored Him, denied Him, and ran from Him, but He never left me. He saw my three brothers and me safely through those years, while many of my friends died. Every time I go back to Woodstock, I walk through my high school and look at the pictures on the walls of my friends and schoolmates who gave their lives for our freedom. It makes me sad, but proud, when I am reminded of the sacrifices that so many made for freedom.

Woodstock was never the same after the war. So many never came home—why them and not us? Was it my mother's prayers?

Romance in Woodstock

The war in Europe ended in May 1945, and I volunteered for duty in the Pacific. All who were heading for the Pacific were given a thirty-day furlough before we left. I went home for the month.

Just after arriving in Woodstock, I was downtown doing a little shopping, and Joan and a friend walked by. We talked, and she invited me to a party that night at her house. Of course I went and we had a great time. In fact, we had such a good time that we had a date every night of my thirty-day leave! That was the big band era—a time for dances, parties, and concerts in the park; a time for falling in love.

While I was busy romancing Joan, America dropped the bomb on Japan and the war in the Pacific was over. I reported back at the end of my leave and was soon discharged. I returned to Woodstock and my jobs: an order expeditor at LaFrance Textiles during the week and a meat cutter at Lynch's Meat Market on Saturdays. Joan had escaped a bad home situation by taking a job in London about thirty miles from Woodstock. Every night when I got off work, I caught the train to London to go and see her. I always tried to make the last train back to

Woodstock, but usually missed it and ended up hitchhiking home after midnight. I didn't care. I was in love.

Married in Woodstock

In October, Joan came to Woodstock for a weekend visit and we got engaged. We were so excited. I gave her an engagement ring, and she went home to tell her parents. Her parents ate dinner at six o'clock sharp every night, and Joan barely made it into her chair on time. Then, just as they began passing the food, she put out her left hand and said to her mom and dad, "Look what I just got." Instead of joining in her excitement, her father rapped her on the knuckles with a knife handle, as he had done many times before, and said, "There's to be no talking at this dinner table!" His cruelty hurt far more than his daughter's knuckles.

We set a June wedding date, but Joan's family remained adamantly against the marriage. Her father spoke to me bluntly, telling me this did not have his approval and asking me how on earth I thought I was going to support her on the seven dollars a week I was making. He even came to our house and tried to convince my mother to pressure me into calling it off. For Joan's parents, this was a matter of status and appearances. They didn't want their daughter marrying the son of an Irish scrub woman from the other side of the tracks. They thought Joan could do much better than that.

My own mother could have had a stronger reason to oppose our marriage. Joan was not a Christian, and my mother wanted me to marry a Christian girl. I think we broke her heart, but she never did anything to interfere and always treated Joan very well. I wish she could have lived long enough to see Joan come to the Lord, but my mother died just a year after my marriage, a month before she was to return to Ireland. With all her children grown and out of the nest, she had made plans to go home. Instead, she went to her real home in heaven.

Family opposition aside, there was one practical obstacle to our marriage—housing was impossible to find in Woodstock. It was just after the war and apartments were scarce. LaFrance Textiles did own an apartment building and by a miracle, one of their tenants was moving out in February. I asked Mr. Knechtel for the apartment, and he gave it to me. Joan and I decided that there wasn't much sense in paying rent and not living in the apartment, so we moved our wedding date up three months to March 9.

Our wedding was small, but just right with close friends and family. Joan's parents did not help her in any way with the wedding, but they did come. After the ceremony, we took the train to Paris, Ontario, for a nice dinner with our entire wedding party. Then Joan and I went on to Hamilton for our one-night honeymoon. On Monday I was back at work. A year later, we made it to Niagara Falls for a real honeymoon.

Joan got a secretarial job at Ralston Purina in Woodstock, and we had fun setting up our little apartment, beginning our life together. I did have a few adjustments to make, however. One night I laid my shoes out, and Joan asked me what I was doing. I said, "Well, aren't you going to polish them?" She answered, "Polish them?" I told her that my mother always polished my shoes, and she quickly reminded me that she wasn't my mother, thus initiating our first fight. In the morning my shoes remained where I had left them, unpolished. I also left my pants lying on the floor, expecting Joan to pick them up and iron them for me just like my mother did. Soon I had to pick them up because I only had two pairs and I had to wear something to work. I learned fast that there was a major difference between a wife and a mother.

Despite these minor adjustments, we stayed in love and had a good time. We had many friends, young couples like ourselves, and had an active social life. I played basketball for the YMCA men's league. Joan and the other wives followed us all over Ontario as we played in tournaments. I got involved in the Y's service organization, and Joan joined the women's association. There were Joan's bingo parties and my beer-drinking poker parties. We raced to hockey games in the winter and baseball games in the summer. We went dancing, played cards, and partied, sometimes all night long. We were on the run, and deep inside I knew that what I was really running from was the Lord.

Every once in a while I got this pang of guilt about how I was living. I even talked to Joan about her need to "get saved." I thought that if she became a Christian everything would be easier for me, but she could never understand what I was talking about. Joan was as religious as you could get. She was a moral, church-going woman, and all I could do was talk to her about her need to be "saved." "Saved from what? I can swim," she would say. "I'm not drowning!"

Within a year of our marriage we were able to buy our first house. I had picked up a third job as a ticket taker at the Green Grotto Dance Hall on Thursday nights to earn some extra money for the house. By then, Joan was not working. She had quit her job when her boss would not let her bring a radio to work to listen to the World Series! But it was just as well. She spent her time making our new house into a home. We were so excited and proud and we loved our little house and our new neighbors. Then, in 1948, our first child, Andrea, was born. Ever since I was a boy, I had dreamed of having a home and a family, and now my dream was coming true. It wasn't long after Andrea was born that Joan began talking seriously about moving to the States. For years she had dreamed of living there and had talked about it ever since I had known her. I couldn't really understand her strong desire. I loved Woodstock. Compared to Ireland, it seemed like heaven to me. I had planned to live out my life there. But over the months, Joan's desire to move to America became an intense passion.

The American Dream

Lee Forbes, a Canadian friend who had lived in Texas for many years, was Joan's United States connection. Lee and her husband had moved to Austin, Texas, struck it rich in the oil business, and purchased a number of hotels. After her husband died, Lee returned to Woodstock and lived with Joan's aunt and uncle next door to Joan's house. Lee was blind from glaucoma, so Joan went by each afternoon to read her mail to her and write letters. Through these letters Joan got to know a number of people in Austin. Even after Lee's death, Joan continued her correspondence with these people and wanted to go and meet them. But in the late forties it was not easy to get to the States.

The first step in emigrating was to find a sponsor. We asked my brother Bill, who was living in the Boston area, if he would give me a job and sponsor us. He agreed. The next step was to get a visa. Joan applied under the Canadian emigration quota and I under the Irish. There were long waiting lists for both. It took us a year to get our visas, but they finally arrived on March 17, 1950, St. Patrick's Day. We partied all night with our friends to celebrate.

Within two weeks, we had sold our house and all of our furniture and were on the train to America. We had two thousand dollars in our pockets and thought we were rich. We crossed into America at Buffalo, New York, and continued on to my brother's home, where I began working at his mill. However, within just a few weeks, it was obvious that there were some problems. Things weren't working out the way we had planned. Deciding that this would be a good time to go to Texas to visit Joan's friends, we bought ourselves a 1947 Nash, put our cedar chest, mirror, and two year old in the back seat, and took off.

On the way we stopped by Washington, D. C. to do some sightseeing. The Capitol, the Jefferson and Lincoln Memorials, the White House—it was hard to believe we were actually in America. It would have been even harder to believe the dreams that would come true for us in this land of the free and home of the brave.

"America, the land we love, is still the land of opportunity and freedom. We are ever grateful to those who sacrificed so much so we might have liberty."

ANDY HORNER

❧

"God bless America. Let's not forget that her greatness is not in her intellectualism, technology, or natural resources, but in her people."

ANDY HORNER

❧

CHAPTER FOUR

Deep in the Heart of Texas

t was May of 1950 when we crossed into Texas. It was suddenly very hot, and Joan loved it. She immediately felt like she belonged there. Perhaps she had such strong feelings because God knew this was where we would live and where Joan would find Him.

Not Just a Coincidence

The people in Austin couldn't have been nicer to three refugees from the far North. Lee Forbes' friends, the ones Joan knew only by letter writing, gave us a warm Texas welcome and took us under their wings. One couple let us live in an apartment on the second floor of their house, and we set about finding jobs. Joan found work right away as a bookkeeper at a ladies' wear store downtown, but I could not find a job anywhere. No one wanted to hire an immigrant. Finally, after several weeks, I was hired for very low wages to run a mimeograph machine at the State Highway Department.

I reported to work the following Monday, and no one was there. I sat on the steps of the government building and tried to figure out why everyone had disappeared. I soon discovered it was a holiday, Memorial Day, and no one had remembered to tell me not to come in to work! Angry and discouraged, I decided that we should drive up to Dallas to go to a baseball game that evening. We found Burnett Field just inside the city limits and got a motel room close by.

A neighbor of ours in Woodstock, Bert Blair, had told us that if we ever got to Dallas, we should call his brother. From the motel Joan started calling all the Blairs in the Dallas phone book, asking them if they had a brother in Canada. An hour later, when she got to the very last Blair—William T.—his wife, Mary, screamed out, "Yes, my husband has a brother in Canada!" We made arrangements to meet them the next morning and then went on to the ball game. (Just for the record, I want it noted that on our first night in Dallas, I took Joan to a baseball game—and I am still doing it fifty years later!)

At 7:30 the next morning, Bill Blair knocked on our door. I told him what had happened in Austin, and he immediately took charge. He took me to get a Social Security card, took me to an employment agency, and got me a job at Gillette Motor Freight. He accomplished all of this before noon! I went back to the motel and asked Joan if she wanted to stay in Dallas, and she immediately said yes. Bill found us an efficiency apartment to rent, so we were set. We drove down to Austin, packed up our stuff, thanked the friends who had been so generous and kind, and moved to Dallas—just like that.

What a series of coincidences! Joan's strong desire to come to America, the quick stop in Boston, welcomed by strangers in Austin, the futile job search, a trip to Dallas on a whim to see a baseball game, and wham! Suddenly a friend manages to set everything up and gives a young couple that precious gift called *opportunity*. We never wanted to return to Canada. We never doubted our decision to move to America. And when we landed in Dallas, we knew we were home. Was all this coincidence, or was an unseen hand gently nudging us in His direction?

Learning the Basics in the Office

In Canada I made about eighty dollars a month working three jobs. At Gillette Motor Freight I started at forty dollars a week. Joan and I felt like Texas millionaires. After I'd been working about a month, Bill came by and said that the company where he worked, Allen Engineering, needed an office manager. He thought I should apply for the job. I knew nothing about management. My only experience in an office was at LaFrance Textiles. But Bill said I could do it and he got me hired. This was in July of 1950.

The job at Allen Engineering was the best thing that could have happened to me. It threw me into a crash course in American business, and I was determined to succeed. Like playing athletics as a kid, what I lacked I made up for by plain old hard work. My mother's training paid off. I always did more than I had to, and my bosses noticed. Bill took me under his wing, mentored me, and was proud of everything I accomplished. God partially answered my boyhood prayer for a father in Bill Blair.

I left Allen Engineering after about a year. Mr. Allen was going through a divorce (his third), and the court called me to testify. On the stand I had to say some things that cost my boss more alimony than he wanted to pay. After the trial, I decided it might be best for me to leave. Again it was time to locate another job. The Texas Employment Commission provided a list of possibilities, and I went out on all kinds of interviews. The first one was at a sausage packing factory. What a smell! I learned to thank God for closed doors.

One day at the Employment Commission I overheard a counselor telling her client about an office manager's job at S. C. Johnson and Son (Johnson Wax) that required a college degree. I had dropped out of high school and had no college credits, but this didn't deter me. I drove to Johnson Wax and interviewed with Mr. Lansford, the regional manager. He told me he was considering a candidate who had a degree from Notre Dame, but he was still making up his mind.

I knew I could handle the job and I wanted it. As I left the building, I introduced myself to all the ladies in the office. Every day I went to check if Mr. Lansford had hired anyone yet, and when I did, I stopped to talk to the women, asking about their families and getting to know them. After about a week of this, Mr. Lansford decided that he would let the women in the office decide who they wanted to be their boss. They unanimously said, "That nice young man from Canada," and I was hired. It pays to pay attention to the working women!

I like to tell this story because I think it demonstrates the power of building relationships. I did not have the experience they wanted or the education they required, but I genuinely liked people and could get along with almost anyone. The ability to relate and to lead was something I worked on even as a boy. I think that this love for people, and my mother's faithful prayers, have been major keys in my success.

Mr. Lansford was demanding, hard to work for, and almost impossible to please. I resented him and decided that he exemplified everything I didn't want to be as a manager. But he taught me many things nobody else had the courage to even mention: "Andy, you stink! Use deodorant!" and "Why don't you wear an undershirt under your dress shirt?" These personal care issues were things no one told me as a poor kid in Woodstock. Mr. Lansford showed me how to present myself as a business-man, how to run official meetings, and he taught me prop-er etiquette. He embarrassed me, frustrated me, and made me angry, but I discovered that sometimes the people we like the least teach us the most.

Discovering and Recovering Spiritual Life

Joan and I began to get established in Dallas. We found a good preschool for Andrea, and Joan got a job with the Reserve Life Insurance Company downtown. Some of the women she worked with became good friends, especially Marie Hunter. They started talking to their Canadian friend about coming to their church. Still in my backslidden state, church was the last place I want-ed to be. Besides, these people were liberal Southern Baptists. I had heard all about their kind in Woodstock—these women wore lipstick and cut their hair. Some of them even smoked! I piously told Joan we shouldn't asso-ciate with any of them, but of course the real reason I resisted was that I didn't like the voice that kept speaking to me deep inside. I had been able to stay away from any-thing having to do with God. The only time I brought Him into the picture was when Joan and I had a fight. I would tell her that I was going to heaven and she was going to hell because she wasn't saved. You can imagine the effect of this kind of witness.

In spite of my objections, Joan liked these ladies and wanted to visit their church. So where do you think we went? I found the biggest Bible I could find and tucked it under my arm. Surely no one would bother me if I carried the family Bible. We found the church and got settled in the pew without incident. But then the pastor got up to welcome the visitors. "We are so honored today to have Brother and Sister Horner here with us from Canada. Brother Horner would you please come up here and lead us in the invocation?" I couldn't believe it. I gave Joan an elbow and an angry look before I went up front and prayed. I hadn't been in a church for over ten years, but I remembered the art, and the right words came out loud and clear. Andy Horner did his social thing—what a phony.

When we got home, I decided that I would take care of this church thing once and for all. "Joan, no more church! Period! I've had it. I will never darken the door of a church again!" Of course, the women at Joan's work didn't know of my firm words to Joan. They kept right on inviting her to church, and she kept right on accepting their invitations. I lost my temper, but to no avail. When Joan makes a promise, she keeps it. So where do you think I ended up several more times? I made many passionate speeches insisting that our church career was over, but then even the calendar turned against me. It was the Easter season.

Because Joan was a religious person, she was in the habit of going to church on Good Friday and Easter. She knew better than to ask me, so instead she went with her friend Marie to the noon service on Good Friday, led by Dr. W. A. Criswell at the Palace Theater. The service touched Joan deeply, and she cried during most of it. This was the first time she recalls recognizing that something was missing in her life, that something was seriously wrong.

On Easter Sunday, Billy Graham was preaching in Fort Worth. The year before we had heard him speak in Boston. That time, I went because of mistaken identity. I thought Joan was taking me to see Billy Graham, the prize fighter. In the meantime Billy, the evangelist, had become quite well known, and this was his last weekend in Fort Worth. I could tell that Joan really wanted to go, and since it was Easter, I agreed to take her.

We sat on the top row of the stadium, about as far away as you could get from the speaker, but Billy's message reached us. When he pointed his finger and said, "God is calling you," I felt like he was pointing right at me. Joan was confused. What did Billy mean when he talked about knowing Christ, and why were all these people walking down to the front? I knew what was going on, and all I wanted was to get out of there.

About a month later, in late April, we got a Monday night visit from another of Joan's coworkers, Mrs. Ritchie, a member of First Baptist Church of Dallas. She was an older lady doing church visitation with a gentleman from the church. They came in, sat down, and talked with us about their church, their pastor Dr. Criswell, and how she would love for us to come visit. Just to get her out of my home, I said we might visit sometime. Her response? "Well, how about this Sunday?" I told her that we couldn't make it this Sunday, but maybe some other time. Then Mrs. Ritchie proceeded to explain that this was going to be a very special Sunday. They were having a special convocation and were trying to get as many people to come as possible. Joan thought it was some kind of contest and that our presence could help Mrs. Ritchie win a prize. "We'll be there on Sunday!" she said.

I couldn't believe it. As soon as Mrs. Ritchie left, I told Joan there was no way we were going to that church. I had repeatedly said, "*No more church*," and that was that. Joan argued back, "But I promised we would be there! We've got to go! It wouldn't be fair to Mrs. Ritchie if we didn't."

The next Sunday morning, April 29, 1951, the telephone woke us up at 7:00 A.M. We had been out late the night before partying, and it was a cool, rainy day—perfect for sleeping in. The call was from Mrs. Ritchie, who was checking to make sure we were coming to church. Joan said, "Yes, of course we are coming." I exploded and gave specific instructions from the other side of the bed. "Joan, make up an excuse, anything, because we are absolutely not going." Mrs. Ritchie, unaware of my frantic objections, offered to come and pick us up. Joan said no, we had a car and would meet her there. We found out later that she had no car. She would have had to borrow one. She was simply determined to eliminate every excuse we made and get us there.

When Joan hung up, the war began. I insisted that we were not going. "I'm the head of the home. No way! We're not going." Joan insisted we were obligated. The battle raged. We climbed out of bed, got dressed, and got into the car. Evidently the Lord had been planning this appointment for quite some time.

We arrived downtown and walked into the First Baptist Church. The place was huge, the largest church I had ever seen. The first thing they did was put Andrea in the nursery. Then they took us into the 2,700-seat sanctuary. Both of us were a little nervous. They whisked Joan away to the women's class on one side of the auditorium, while I went to the men's class on the other. Here we were separated in this gigantic church, and then Dr. Criswell stood to speak.

He quoted John 3:16 and preached an evangelistic message that morning. He spoke for just ten minutes. It could qualify as his shortest sermon ever. But in those moments he made the gospel simple and understandable. When the invitation started, hundreds began to go down to the front. I was struggling. I knew I had to get right with God, but I kept fighting it. I didn't know where Joan was or what she was thinking about all this, but I started praying, "God, please save Joan. It will be too hard to live for You if she isn't a Christian. If you will just save Joan, then I will submit to You." I stood there praying for Joan, but I knew that I needed to get right with God myself.

Across the auditorium Joan was having her own struggle. She had always been taught that Jesus was the Savior of the whole world, but she didn't understand what His death had to do with her individual life. She was a very religious, moral woman. Why did she need to be forgiven? Why all this talk about sin and separation from God? Why did God's Son have to die?

Dr. Criswell stopped the singing and had everyone get down on their knees and pray. It was then that Joan began to see that her religious performance could never pay the penalty for her sin. She understood that she was separated from God, that Jesus had taken the punishment she deserved, and that now there was something He wanted her to do. She needed to personally respond to Him and accept Him as her Lord and Savior.

Joan told the Lord that she did not want to be apart from Him. She would accept His offer and allow Him to forgive her and enter her life. Immediately she felt clean. She got up and walked down toward the front, not exactly sure why she was going there.

I had no idea what Joan was doing, but I couldn't hold out any longer. I knew I had to rededicate my life to the Lord with or without Joan. I moved out into the aisle and began making my way to the front. I came down the right side and the instant I arrived, I saw Joan coming from the left. I walked toward her and we met in the middle. Our lives have been united with Christ since that moment. We were both totally changed.

"If you want favor with both God and man, and a reputation for good judgment and common sense, then trust the Lord completely; don't ever trust yourself."

PROVERBS 3:4-5, TLB

❦

"You can be persuaded that whatever we commit unto the Lord, He is able to keep. This is a great fact."

ANDY HORNER

❦

CHAPTER FIVE

The Fabulous Fifties

We knew that our lives had definitely changed. Our relationship improved. We still got angry at each other sometimes, but the outbursts of temper with all the yelling, screaming, and throwing things at one another ended. Our social calendar definitely changed as our lives became focused on growing in the Lord. Most of our activities began to revolve around First Baptist Church.

Spiritual Baby Steps at First Baptist

One of the first things Joan wanted to do after she became a Christian was to get baptized. I couldn't understand why she would want to do such a thing or why she thought she needed to. I couldn't talk her out of it and couldn't explain things very well, so I decided that we should meet with Dr. Criswell and talk about it.

We made an appointment and went to his office. He listened to our testimonies and then talked to us about some first steps in our new Christian life. He stressed the importance of obeying Christ, and that the first step of obedience was to be baptized. He told us that Jesus

Himself walked miles over rough terrain to the Jordan to set the example. Dr. Criswell said that it must be the Holy Spirit prompting Joan to want to be baptized because she had not been taught about it, had never even seen an adult baptism, and certainly her husband hadn't told her to do this. He told me that I should not hold her back if this is what God was leading her to do.

This meeting with Dr. Criswell was strategic for Joan and me; that was the day he truly became our pastor. His gentle and sweet teaching encouraged us, and we have loved him dearly ever since. He baptized Joan on the following Sunday, May 13, 1951.

We immediately got involved in the programs of First Baptist Church. We joined a Training Union group (that was the Sunday night activity) and got to know a lot of other young couples. We made many lifelong friends and had a great time together. Joan joined a women's Sunday school class that was taught by Mary Crowley. If Dr. Criswell was Joan's spiritual father, Mary Crowley became her spiritual mother. Mary came to our apartment in the afternoons and taught Joan about the Bible. She started at the beginning and took Joan through the Bible chronologically, teaching her the stories and giving her an overview of the Scriptures and of God's plan. Joan had always been an excellent student and she was eager to study. She grew quickly as a Christian.

Mary also taught Joan how to pray. With Andrea down for a nap, Mary and Joan would kneel beside an old chair in our living room. Joan could sense Mary's deep faith and she learned from Mary that there was nothing too big or too small about which to ask God. One of Joan's first prayer requests was to get pregnant. We had been trying for some time to have a second child but with no success. Then, in May 1952, Sarah was born—proof to us that God does listen and answer our prayers. Once the Lord got started, He just kept pouring on the blessings. Tim was born in December 1953, Mary in April 1956, and Tommy in August 1958. In very short order, we went from one child to five!

On a return trip to Woodstock, Joan learned the source of her spiritual hunger. We were visiting Oxford Street Church, where I had attended for so many years, when a Mrs. Whitehead came up to Joan and asked her if Cecily knew that she had become a Christian. The only Cecily that Joan knew was Cecily Hardwicke, her nanny from the time she was born until she was six. Mrs. Whitehead said, "Yes, that's the one. You must call her."

Joan went home from church and immediately called Cecily. She identified herself and explained that Mrs Whitehead told her to call and let her know that she had become a Christian. Sobbing with joy, Cecily said that she had been praying for Joan for thirty years. Joan was amazed as Cecily told her of the choruses she had sung to her, the Bible stories she had told her, and how she had talked about Jesus as she pushed Joan in her stroller. It was clear that God had been at work in Joan's life since her earliest years through this loving, faithful Christian nanny.

All during this time, our family life and social life revolved around the First Baptist Church. We were active in Sunday school and Training Union, soon taking on teaching and leadership responsibilities. Joan joined a WMU (Women's Missionary Union) circle and attended Bible studies. I was elected to the Junior Board and became a deacon. We went to Sunday morning service, Sunday school, Training Union, Sunday evening service, and Wednesday night prayer meeting. The kids were in

Sunday school, Training Union, Sunbeams, GA's (then, Girl's Auxiliary; today, Girls in Action), RA's (Royal Ambassadors), choirs, Vacation Bible School—whatever was going on, we were there, often four and five days a week. At the same time, I was grabbing for the next rungs on the corporate ladder.

A Chance for the Top

These were the fifties—the days of *Ozzie and Harriet, Leave It to Beaver,* and *Walt Disney*—and my role as bread-winner was to work hard and keep bringing home a lot more than bacon. I eagerly climbed the corporate ladder at Johnson Wax, honing my skills and making a reputation for myself in the company. My job performance was good and I was getting very nice raises and bonuses—so much so that in 1952, Joan and I were able to buy a nice three-bedroom home, and in 1956, to build our "dream house" with four bedrooms, two baths, and a family kitchen! Then the big break came.

In early 1959, Mr. Lansford mentioned to me that there was a job opening at company headquarters in Racine, Wisconsin. He thought I was qualified and he had put my name in for the job. "Andy, you're a talented and motivated young man," he told me. "This is a big opportunity. I think you should pursue it." My head swelled three hat sizes. A job at the home office! Here I was, a poor kid from Belfast who started with nothing, living the American dream.

Without much thought and virtually no investigation, I took the promotion and made plans for us to move to Wisconsin. If I had known then what I know now, I would not have been so hasty. I never honestly consulted Joan and certainly didn't seriously consider her or the kids' wishes. To me, and probably to most other men of that era, it was a given that I would grab such an opportunity. This was my goal as a working man. The point was to make it to the top of the company. This proved you were a good provider for your family and a husband any wife would be proud of. And I was on my way!

After getting the promotion, I moved immediately to Racine leaving Joan in Dallas, pregnant, with five kids, to organize the family move by herself. I threw myself into the important thing—my new job as Assistant to the Marketing Vice President. The headquarters were beautiful and new, designed by Frank Lloyd Wright, and just being there was heady stuff. I was oblivious to any family problems. However, before Joan could move to Racine, she had a miscarriage. In retrospect, I believe that this miscarriage resulted partly from the emotional and physical stress related to having to leave Dallas and organize the move by herself.

Not too many weeks later, I loaded Joan and the kids into the station wagon and moved them to Racine. Joan was still not well. She spent her first few weeks in Wisconsin in the hospital. The kids were crammed into a two-bedroom apartment while our new house was being finished. They were literally living out of boxes and eating on top of them, adjusting to new schools and new friends, all without Joan—and me working my way to the top.

Some wonderful Christian people from the Racine Bible Church saw to it that dinner was provided every night. They helped with the kids, the cleaning, and the laundry. Of course, when Joan was home and well enough, the first church we wanted to visit was Racine Bible. We got very involved and had a lot of fun trying to loosen those somber Yankees up, getting them to take some risks as a church, and step out on faith. The pastor, Phil Whisen-hunt, had studied at Dallas Theological Seminary and some of Texas had rubbed off on him. We loved him and his family and made many other dear friends. Church and a few friends were the only good things for Joan in the north. She hated the cold, the snow, and the reserve of the people. She was depressed by her surroundings and she missed Dallas, Dr. Criswell, her friends, and the hot weather.

One New Year's, Joan was so homesick that she decided to go to Dallas for Dr. Criswell's New Year's Eve service. We drove to Chicago so she and our three youngest could catch the train, but all the seats were sold. Joan was determined to get there one way or another, so I paid a porter to let her sit in a restroom—and that's where she and the kids rode, all the way to Dallas!

I performed well at Johnson Wax and was promoted again, this time to National Administration Manager. This position gave me more responsibility and placed me on critical management committees. I learned a lot about how corporate managers think and plan, and was exposed to the inner operations of the company. Johnson Wax was a well organized and well-managed company. It provided a wonderful opportunity to learn valuable management lessons. I learned the importance of company image, and how vital it is to maintain a good company name. They pounded home the message of quality and service, and how hard a company must work to maintain that quality and service.

But there was also a disillusioning side. Some of the luster of corporate headquarters began to fade. I learned how to play corporate games—how to be politic and flatter others. It was my responsibility to write the minutes for the management committee meetings, and I saw how my bosses altered the minutes to say only what they wanted them to say; how they manipulated others to make sure their own positions were secure and to cover up mistakes. I watched—and I learned how to do it, too. I saw myself becoming more like the men I worked for and beginning to violate my own principles. It made me uncomfortable. Working at company headquarters wasn't what I had expected it would be, and it certainly wasn't what I thought it should be. I hardly recognized some of the basic lessons God was teaching me to prepare for what He had planned down the road.

With my growing disillusionment and Joan's persisting unhappiness, I began to think about doing something else. Joan ran across a newspaper ad for a business for sale in the small east Texas town of Gladewater and investigated it. I had always dreamed of going into business for myself and this looked like a good opportunity. It was a little office supply business that was doing well enough to support us. The owner was selling the business and a nice brick house together in one deal. I thought this would be a good place for the kids to grow up. It also got us back to Texas, only two hours from Dallas. I knew Joan would be pleased.

I made an offer that the owner, Homer Dennis, accepted. Immediately we made plans to move, while at the same time planning ways to expand the business. I struck a deal with Johnson Wax to carry their complete line of janitorial supplies and in one stroke set up a distribution center for east Texas. "A & J Office and Janitorial Supplies" was born.

A Chance for Our Own Business

We moved from Racine in the summer of 1962. We were sad to leave some of the people, but we were also glad to be going home to Texas. We settled into our new home and began establishing roots in the city. We attended the First Baptist Church of Gladewater. Joan was involved in women's clubs and with the kids' schools. I became active in civic clubs and traveled. I spent much of my time on the road drumming up new business for the janitorial supplies while Joan kept the store going. I was uniquely qualified to be selling janitorial supplies, of course, and did very well at demonstrating how to scrub and wax floors. I'd had years of practice at my mother's knee—literally!

The business slowly grew and our selling radius expanded. But I had never worked so hard for so little in my life. Joan and I were both putting in sixty-plus-hour weeks and we were getting tired. We also didn't have much time for a decent family life, and we missed that. The only way we could get any time off was to hang a sign on the door saying we were at a funeral. Members of our families died in droves during those two years—some even died twice!

A Chance to Return to Big D

Although we were back in Texas, a huge improvement, Joan still longed to live in Dallas and return to the First Baptist Church and her pastor. She didn't close the drapes and sit in a dark house depressed as she had done in Racine, but she still missed Dr. Criswell's preaching and wanted the kids involved in the programs at First Baptist. We occasionally drove the eighty miles to Dallas on Sundays to go to church and see friends. This only made her miss it more.

In early 1963, Joan was again up to her practice of placing newspaper ads on my dresser. This time the ad was for a job with the Xerox Corporation. They were building a new regional distribution center and were looking for a manager. Guess where they wanted to place this center? Now I knew nothing about Xerox. In fact, I thought it was the antifreeze company. But I sent in my resume anyway, just for the fun of it, and then forgot about it.

Months later, I was surprised when I received a call from Andy Price of Xerox. It took me a few seconds to realize what he was calling about. He asked me to drive to Dallas and interview for the position I had applied for months earlier. I figured I had nothing to lose, so I did the interview. I was called back for two more interviews over the next three months. I was tested and evaluated by the company psychologist, Dr. Smith. He and I developed a wonderful relationship and he was very helpful in many ways. He helped me to understand myself better and to see why I did the things I did. He helped me see that I needed to relax and accept the fact that everyone has weaknesses, including me, and there was no need to try to hide them. He also counseled that probably I would be happier as a big fish in a little pond, than as a little fish in a big pond. Despite getting to know me so well, he must have decided I wasn't too crazy because I was offered the job in the fall of 1963.

Joan and I decided that I should take the position. She remained in Gladewater running the business until it sold. I moved up to Irving and lived in a rented house until the family joined me in January of 1964.

Xerox was a good company and the job was an excellent opportunity. I oversaw the completion of the new Dallas distribution center and organized the warehousing and distribution of parts and equipment for the entire Southwest. This kind of task was right down my alley and I liked the challenge of it. During these years, Xerox was growing and expanding rapidly. My region kept up so well with the growth that I was sent to other distribution centers in the United States and in Canada to analyze the organization and come up with recommendations to improve operations. It was exciting.

Of course, not everything about any job is all good. One of the drawbacks to working at Xerox at this time was that such rapid growth brought frequent changes in policy. Every time a new person became president or vice president of some division, things changed. Sometimes the changes came down so fast that it was hard to keep up. We would be in the process of implementing one set of changes as another new set was handed down. Projects would be canceled with no warning and no explanation. Once, we were in the process of opening a machine replacement center in Dallas. We had leased the building and hired the staff, only to be told that the center was being shut down. We were closed down before we even opened up! I have to admit that this Irishman got frustrated more than once.

In general, though, I was happy. My job was good and taught me one very important lesson: It is vital to support your product and serve your customers if you want to sustain growth. I saw time and time again how Xerox beat the competition because we could service the customer better, quicker, and more efficiently. My experience convinced me that *serving* and *supporting* was the key, a principle that I have never forgotten.

After a few years, I had the distribution center running so efficiently that I ended up with a lot of time to play golf and get bored. Now I hate doing nothing, because you never know when you're done. I looked to other challenges instead and got involved in various civic organizations. I was elected president of the Rotary Club and chaired the Community Chest drive. Xerox encouraged their managers to do these kinds of things, so they were pleased and I enjoyed it.

Years earlier, Johnson Wax had encouraged me to continue my education, and had paid for me to attend classes two or three nights a week at Southern Methodist University in Dallas. My college degree was on hold when we moved to Racine, but now back in Dallas, I pursued my education again. I had never thought of myself as college material, and I am sure that my teachers and principals in Canada never did either. This was one time my "hyperactivity" was a positive thing. It gave me energy to burn and an ability to do several things all at once. Because of my hectic schedule, I needed help. My college degree was a family affair. Without Joan's support and my daughter Andrea's tutoring, I would not have made it. I graduated from college the same day Andrea graduated from high school.

Joan and I again immersed ourselves at First Baptist and maintained a breakneck pace of activities and raising our five kids. The kids were into everything—church, school, and especially sports. We enjoyed getting to be a part of it all. We tried our best never to miss a performance or a game. We also were back to teaching Sunday school and leading a Training Union department. We developed outreach ministries in our neighborhood. Joan taught two Bible study classes a week—one for young married women and one for more mature women—and we had a couples' Bible class in our home once a week for our neighbors, nicknamed "the Humble-ites." Combine all this with a monthly dinner club with church friends, along with extensive camping and boating, and you've got a very active social and family calendar.

These were great years, but they were also too busy. Often I felt tired and weary. At times I felt like quitting everything. The Horners are a wandering, rootless group by nature and the temptation was there. If it were not for Joan and the five kids, I think I might have drifted away. But the responsibility of a wife, five children, and a home kept me disciplined at my work. I certainly didn't have much internal peace or joy, but I stayed with it regardless of how I felt. Dads and husbands weren't supposed to quit in the fifties and early sixties. Feeling fulfilled and discerning my life purpose, however, would have to wait for more maturing.

*"Although your road may bend and curve,
And winds blow hard that can disturb,
Keep moving on and you will find
More opportunities and much sunshine."*

ANDY HORNER

❧

*"Difficulties and problems in life can either
be stumbling blocks or stepping stones,
but are always opportunities for growth."*

ANDY HORNER

❧

CHAPTER SIX

The Direct Sales Connection

*I*f the Horner tribe possessed some wanderlust genes, the mid sixties gave me a lot of temptation to activate them. I did, in fact, make an important journey from *wax* to *copiers* to *home decorating*, but it all happened right in Dallas.

From Copiers to Home Decorating

Because of my success in organizing the Dallas Distribution Center, Xerox began offering me other positions and promotions outside of Dallas. But I had learned a lesson—not all that glitters on the corporate staircase to success is gold. I decided I would not move my family again unless all of us agreed.

In 1966, Xerox offered me a job at their corporate headquarters in Rochester, New York. Frigid winds off Lake Erie, piles of snow, and the necessity of moving across the MasonDixon Line—Joan wanted nothing to do with it, and the kids agreed. The Johnson Wax headquarters experience had taught me that a relocation was not necessarily a trip to heaven. But I also knew that if I kept turning down this kind of promotion, my career at Xerox would be placed on hold. Rejecting promotions just wasn't done. It put lack of loyalty, no ambition, and questionable commitment on your resume. I knew that I would no longer be considered a "company man," and the offers would soon stop. I also worried that my job in Dallas might be in jeopardy. I went ahead and turned it down and wondered what the future would hold. At least I had finally learned to put my family ahead of my career. It was about time.

I was surprised when, only a few months later, the company offered me another promotion. Xerox was diversifying into other businesses and had recently acquired a book distribution operation on the West Coast. They asked me to move to California and head up this new division. Ocean and beaches, skiing and surfing, Disneyland and plenty of sunshine—this time Joan and the kids were interested! Joan and I took a couple of trips to California and hunted for houses. We discovered one with a beautiful pool and checked out the nearby churches. We all felt we could be happy there, and everyone was in agreement that this was a good move, so I accepted the position. My replacement was hired and moved to Dallas with his family. I trained him, and we prepared to move to the land of the fruits and the nuts.

I can't believe what happened next. I had accepted the new position, we were packing our things to move, and I was training my replacement; but I had no excitement about the new position. My enthusiasm was zero, and I couldn't sleep at night. I just had no peace about the whole thing. Joan and I did a lot of late-night talking and praying. What in the world was going on with me? Everything was in place for us to go, but I just didn't feel like going. Joan and I decided that if I felt this way, we shouldn't move.

I called company headquarters and told them I had changed my mind. I told them that I had decided to stay in Dallas and not take the California job after all. I didn't know how they would react, but they generously offered me my old job back. I stayed on, but decided that it would be wise to start looking for a job with a Dallas-based company. I didn't ever want to face the prospect of moving again!

The Home Interiors Experience

One of my friends suggested that I talk to Mary Crowley who knew many business people and might know of some openings in Dallas. Joan and I remembered Mary, of course. In our early years in Dallas, she had been Joan's Sunday school teacher and had helped Joan take her first steps of growth in the Lord. We loved and respected her deeply, but we had lost touch with her. I didn't even know she had her own company, Home Interiors and Gifts. I thought that it wouldn't hurt to get back in contact with her and see if she might know of some open doors.

I made an appointment and went to Mary's office. It was good to see her again and we had a pleasant, relaxed conversation. "Andy, give me some of your background and tell me what you would like to do now." I ran through my job history and told her that I was hoping she might be able to give me some referrals. Her next words stunned me. Out of the blue she said, "Andy, I believe you are God's man for Home Interiors. You need to be right here with us."

Mary's words caught me totally off guard. I didn't know what to say. I hadn't even considered this possibility. Besides, I wasn't sure at all that I was the man for her job. This was a direct sales company with about ten thousand women Displayers (independent contractors) selling home decorating accessories. I knew nothing about direct sales or home accessorizing, and I wasn't sure I wanted to get involved in a business with ten thousand women! But Mary insisted that I at least talk to her son, Don Carter, about the possibility of coming to work with them. I agreed to do that much.

Mary set up the appointment, and I arrived right on time. I sat there—waiting and waiting and waiting. After over an hour, I was impatient and frustrated. I believed I knew the scenario: Don's mother was probably making him talk to me, and he did not share her belief that I was needed at Home Interiors. When we finally spoke, I got the distinct feeling that he wasn't interested in talking with me about anything. We had a very short visit, and I got up and left. The Horner pride still needed some down-sizing.

Mary was in Europe during this botched appointment episode. When she heard what had happened, she sent me an airgram asking me not to make any decision until she got back. She reconfirmed that she was sure that I was God's man for Home Interiors. By the time she returned I had begun applying for other jobs, but Mary would not let it go. She was the most persistent and determined lady I have ever known. She stayed on me, even visiting our home to try and convince me. When she got to our place, she looked around and said, "Why all these blank walls? A home just should not be this empty! Your walls need some loving." The next thing I knew, she was back with boxes full of decorating items. She completely accessorized our house! And it was awesome. I saw firsthand what a difference accessories could make in a home. She had convinced me about her product and the service she offered.

As she continued to talk with me, I was also intrigued by the direct sales angle and Mary's philosophy of business.

Still, a major doubt lingered. How would I fit in with a mother-son leadership team? I just didn't see Home Interiors in my future. However, Mary wouldn't take no for an answer. She asked me in July of 1967 if I would come in the evenings after my workday at Xerox to do what I could to help out.

Just as Mary had thought, there was some room for improvement. The sales organization was doing fine and was growing rapidly. But because of the rapid growth in the field, the warehouse and home office systems were lagging behind, unable to service and support the field the way it deserved. It was apparent that if they didn't get those elements in line, the continued growth of the company was in jeopardy.

After about six months, I received a call from Don asking if he could meet with me. I agreed, but this time I had him come to my Xerox office. I certainly wasn't going to sit again for an hour in his waiting room! Our visit went well. We talked about the growth and expansion of Home Interiors and what kind of things needed to be done to ensure the future. He told me about the family atmosphere of their company and how it differed from Xerox or other corporations. I didn't know where he was coming from that day, but many years later he told me that his mom was so excited about the possibility of getting me that she just didn't let up on him. She told him to go out to Xerox to hire me before someone else snatched me, and even to buy some copier machines in order to get me to come on board! It was his mother's confidence and "feeling of joy about it" that convinced him, he said. He and Mary made me an offer, and I began full-time with Home Interiors in early

1968. Don told me at the time that this would be the best decision I ever made in my life. He was right.

And what about that job in California? The new division that I was to have managed for Xerox was consolidated with a company based in Detroit, Michigan! I believe that there was Someone who loved us very much who gave me those sleepless nights and uneasy feelings. He protected us from a potentially disastrous, short-lived move to the West Coast because He had some very special things in store for us at Home Interiors.

I started at Home Interiors as Don Carter's assistant, overseeing the warehouse and taking over various administrative and organizational duties for Don. I never worked so hard in my life—and I have done a lot of hard work. There was a lot of pressure keeping up with the growing sales force. To add to the stress, I was working for a mother and her son. I tried to please them both, but it was sometimes difficult. I was middle management all right— right in the middle between Mary and her son. At times it was a difficult situation for me, and after only a few months, I thought I had made a big mistake.

I considered quitting many times, but I have never felt right about running away from something difficult. Plus, the money was good. We had one child in college by then and four close behind her. Like most men in midlife, my family responsibilities made me stay, although it was an emotional roller coaster ride the entire seventeen years I was there. God doesn't promise us a relaxing vacation on Waikiki Beach. He had some important lessons for me to learn in the midst of this struggle.

The Mary Crowley School of Wisdom

Mary Crowley worked hard and demanded the same of others, but she was also extremely generous. She always had a moment to look you in the eye, take you by the hand, and ask how you were. She was thoughtful and loving, strong and straightforward, with an unwavering faith in God. Mary firmly believed that *everybody is a somebody.* I can still hear her say, "Andy, you be sure to spread this truth. Tell everybody that they are a somebody; that they can do whatever they set their mind to do. *God did not take time to make a nobody.*" Mary insisted that we see others with eyes of love no matter how difficult and negative they were. "We should always see the person as God sees them, a valued child of God, the person they might be able to become, not necessarily the way they are at this moment."

Mary practiced what she preached. She had a way of looking at you and immediately seeing all that you could do and become. Then she challenged you to do and to become just that. "Think mink," she said, "not rabbit or fox or squirrel. Aim for the best. Attempt great things. Believe big and you'll get big results."

Mary taught me to constantly focus on the people. She told me many times, "Andy, if you build the people, they will build the business. Expect the best from them and they will respond. Meet their needs and they will support you and meet every need in your life." She believed that if you helped other people get what they wanted out of life, then you would get what you wanted out of life. She persistently built this sense of "otherness" into the sales force and all the employees. She taught us how to be alert to the needs of others and how serving others meant more than teaching them about home decorating accessories. "Service is our survival kit. We need to give service in home decorating, but we also need to allow women to air their problems, express their hopes and fears, and help them in whatever ways we can. We will find our highest fulfillment not in beautifying homes but in beautifying lives."

Mary's belief in serving went beyond the customers and the people who did the work. She applied this service to the home office management team. As I worked with her over the years, she transformed my thinking from a *managing others* point of view to a *serving others* point of view. She demonstrated this attitude wherever she went, and I could see the power of it. The more I relaxed and concentrated on ways to serve others and help others, rather than trying to get them to do what I wanted, the better things went for me with people in the field and around the home office. This change in my attitude was needed the most in my relationship with Don and Mary, and I discovered that a spirit of genuine humble service was the key.

Before I met Mary I had always been a people person. But I learned even more about the way people really are from Mary Crowley. She taught me to genuinely appreciate others and to understand that they are the key to success. "People are our most important asset!" she repeated over and over until this hardheaded Irishman got the message into his life.

There's a story about Mary that demonstrates the priority of people over profits. At the end of her first year of business the company was not going to make a huge profit, but it was not in the red either. She decided that she would pay a small dividend on the stock and give bonuses to the home office staff and managers. She called her accountant and told him to draw up the checks. He was appalled and told her that she could not do this, that if she did, she would have no reserve whatsoever. He said that no one expects a dividend or a bonus the first year of a business. Mary replied, "What do you mean we'd have no reserve. It all depends on what you call reserve. *You* say it's money. *I* say it's people." She paid the dividend and the bonuses, and the company went on to increased profits every year after that. Mary understood that people were the key. Investments in people always pay off. In fact, I developed a little motto for Home Interiors: "To most companies, P & L means Profit and Loss. At Home Interiors, it means People and Love."

Partners on the Road

After a short while, I was promoted to Vice President of Administration and was given some very nice bonuses for the work I was doing. Things were running smoothly. We had the systems in place to serve and support the field the way we wanted to, which in turn led to an increase in sales, recruiting, and in company profits.

In the early seventies, Mary and Don noticed that there were some areas of the country that were having special problems and needed extra help. They asked me to travel to these areas and do training, leadership development, and rebuilding. Soon I was doing that kind of work exclusively and was given the title to match: Vice President of People and Area Development.

Joan traveled with me whenever she could. Our kids were grown and out on their own, so she was free to leave home. She was an incredible asset to me personally, as well as to the company. The people loved her, and she developed close, supportive relationships with many of our Displayers and managers in the field. She also began assisting Mary in ways that only a good friend could, to the point of accompanying her on many trips both here and abroad.

By 1976, Joan's role had become so vital that Mary and Don asked her to join Home Interiors on a full-time basis. I was pleased, of course, because I had gotten to the place where I refused to travel without her. We made a good team as we worked with the women in the field. Of all the jobs that I had had up to this point, this was the best fit. Both Joan and I loved developing people and building these new sales areas. We were using all our people skills and saw immediate results where they counted—in the lives of women. I watched their confidence and self-esteem grow as they built their businesses. I saw them develop as leaders and as women. This was gratifying work, but it was not easy. It was demanding and exhausting. We worked long hours and traveled almost weekly across the country. Some days I felt absolutely drained, not wanting to take another phone call or get on another plane. But, then, nothing worthwhile is easy.

A Blowout on the Road

Looking back on those years now, I can hardly believe all that we were doing in addition to our Home Interiors work. We continued to be involved in many ministries at First Baptist Church. We taught Sunday school and led Training Union. I was a deacon and board member. I ushered at many services and often gave the invocation. In the mid-sixties I served on the committee that set up the Criswell Bible Institute, and over the next two decades I lent whatever leadership and assistance I could. Criswell Bible Institute evolved into the Criswell Center for Biblical Studies and then, ultimately, to its present status of the Criswell College. I served on its Board of Trustees for numerous terms and as Board Chairman twice. I was on the original committee that set up KCBI, the college's

Christian radio station, and stayed involved until that ministry was firmly on its feet.

All of these activities were good and worthwhile in themselves, but I was doing them for the wrong reasons and I was wearing myself out "working for Jesus." I equated spirituality with activity. I thought that being a good Christian meant I should be at church every time the doors opened and should serve in whatever capacity I was asked. I didn't comprehend that being a Christian was about a relationship with God, not about a life overly full of Christian activities. I had spent my entire adult life performing for God, and I was getting worn out. There was no joy in any of it for me, and the God that created the world in six days was not that impressed.

I was empty, frustrated, and burning out as a Christian, and I didn't know what to do about it. I thought about standing in front of our church and yelling out, "Hey, folks, I'm tired. I'm weary. I've lost my joy and my peace. I'm not what you think, and I'm so tired of performing as a Christian. I can't do this anymore. I thought Jesus said His yoke was easy. Pulling this load is killing me!"

To increase the burden, the pressures at Home Interiors were building. Delicate interpersonal and legal problems had to be handled, and the situation was stressful. Many days I whispered to myself, *I've got to resign.* But how could I walk away from the big money and the freedom and security I believed it brought? How could Joan and I stop giving so much support to the various missions and ministries that we loved? There were still the children's college bills to pay. Plus, Joan and I enjoyed working together. She was as involved and attached to the people as I was, and she didn't want to leave them or Mary

Crowley. I went to Mary on a number of occasions and tried to resign, explaining that I thought maybe I wanted to pursue full-time Christian work. Each time she told me that I could help others ten times more by giving money to support a number of ministries than I could by going into one ministry myself. Every time I brought up quitting, she talked me out of it. So I stayed and the strain continued to mount.

But by 1982, I was burned out. I was absolutely miserable and almost destroyed myself. I could not go on with things the way they were. I went to Mary and resigned, telling her that I was emotionally depressed and physically exhausted.

For the next year, Joan and I continued to work with a few areas of the country, but as independent consultants to Home Interiors, not employees. In 1984, we made the final break. I was totally burned out and simply couldn't find the energy to continue in any capacity. I started my own consulting company, Management and People Services, and developed a few clients, providing organizational, training, and motivational services to direct selling companies. I felt relieved to be away from the pressure, but the last few years had taken their toll. Desperate and adrift, I struggled with myself and wrestled with God. *Now what? Where do I go from here?* I was losing hope and started seeking answers in every way I knew how.

*"Don't let feelings determine your destiny.
Most of the work in the world is done
by people who don't feel like it."*

ANDY HORNER

⚜

*"Luck in business is equal to preparation
plus hard work plus opportunity."*

ANDY HORNER

⚜

CHAPTER SEVEN

The Birth of Premier Designs

As Joan and I were breaking away from Home Interiors, I began pulling away from the church. For a couple of years I just didn't go. I was totally burned out and simply didn't have the fuel to continue. I resigned my positions and withdrew from my teaching responsibilities. I was miserable, discouraged, and adrift. Lost in a deep emotional bog, I questioned my faith. I questioned God. Where was He? What was faith? What did I believe?

I cringed at the thought that someone might find out that I was actually asking these kinds of questions. People respected me as a fine Christian and church leader. I couldn't let them know I was actually doubting the truth of the whole thing. I couldn't admit to anyone what was really going on inside. No one knew how bad it was or how low I went. Some days I felt so hopeless and weary I just didn't want to go on.

Then gradually, as I cried out to God for answers, the light began to dawn. I began to realize the truth. I had been sweating it out for Jesus all those years, doing everything I could in my own strength to earn His pat on my head and to hear Him say, "Well done!" In fact, it became clear to me that my major concern had been what people thought of me and whether or not they considered me a good Christian. My focus had been horizontal, instead of vertical, and there is nothing more futile than trying to do a supernatural task in plain old natural strength. I had worked so hard to please God that I had forgotten to love Him and to let Him love me! Finally, He decided it was time to enroll me in His course on *Son Dependence*, instead of *Andy Dependence*.

Amazing things began to happen over the next year as I spent time studying the Bible and concentrating on my relationship with God. I began opening up with friends and God provided help and encouragement through them. For example, Bob and Amy George reminded me over and over again that God is not interested in our performance, but loves us as we are. I began to rest and relax as I allowed Jesus to work through me, instead of me working for Him.

I stopped asking internal questions like, "What will the church leaders think of me if I do this?" and started asking, "What does my heavenly Father really want?" Step by step, I started seeing small evidences of His Spirit's fruit in my life. Gradually, peace and joy began to reappear in my heart. It was wonderful—revolutionary! I realized that for sixty years God had tried to get me to relax and let Him sculpt me into what He wanted. But my pride made me resistant clay. I was so busy impressing others with my "spirituality" that I lost sensitivity to the Spirit. It took sixty years for God to really get my full attention. I regret that it took so long, but I am grateful that He never gave up on me. Isn't it wonderful to know that God never quits on one of His kids?

During this time of growing close to the Lord, I started asking God to reveal what He wanted me to do with the rest of my life. I didn't need to work for money, but I did need to work for Him. Besides, I don't believe in retirement. The word should be removed from the dictionary. Heaven is God's retirement center, and it is a lot more plush than Palm Springs or Sarasota. I wasn't about to look for shells in the morning on the beach and then play golf all day until a favorite TV sitcom came on that night. I knew God wanted me to change direction, not retire, and to accomplish a whole new mission. But what direction should I take? This time I wanted Him to take the lead.

The Door Begins to Open

During this period of searching, I was trying to decide if Joan and I should go into full-time ministry. My brother Hugh was a preacher, and I hoped that God would give me that "special call" to be a preacher, too; but it never came. Joan and I thought about going to the mission field or working with a mission organization in some capacity, but no opportunity opened up.

About this same time, two significant things happened. First, I went on a mission trip to Poland with my friend Dave Wyrtzen. We spent twenty-four hours sitting next to each other on airplanes traveling there and back. During that time I took the opportunity to spill my entire life story to him. I shared that I was seeking God's leading and was thinking about becoming a preacher or going to the mission field. But as Dave heard my life experience, he challenged me to take a hard look at my unique personal gifts. "Andy, it's obvious. You're an entrepreneur. In both the corporate world and the world of direct sales, you have received specialized training in how to build a company and how to effectively manage it. Do you think the Lord wants to trash all these skills He has carefully matured in you? Why don't you consider being an entrepreneur for the Lord, a businessman who lives in the marketplace totally at the beck and call of His Master?" *An entrepreneur for Jesus*—the idea intrigued me. This conversation with Dave turned out to be pivotal.

The second major influence came when my daughter Sarah and her family moved to Bolivia, South America as missionaries. Joan and I went to visit them for Christmas in 1984. While we were there, Bob and Ann Moore invited us to come farther south with them to visit Word of Life ministries in Argentina.

Joan and I had met Bob and Ann several years earlier through our good friends Bruce and Maggie Peterson—and we had met Bruce and Maggie through our dear friends from Racine, Don and Marion Placko. Each summer the Plackos attended a Bible conference at Word of Life headquarters in Schroon Lake, New York. For years, they tried to get us to go with them. Finally, in 1974, we were able to go and we loved it. It was there that we became close friends with Bruce and Maggie, and then Bob and Ann. (Though she hates to admit it, Joan says that the Lord was at work even in our move to Racine—where we met the Plackos who introduced us to Word of Life!)

At that particular time, the last thing we wanted to do was to go to Argentina. Joan was ill, and we were planning to cut the Bolivia visit short and go home early. But Bob kept calling and asking us to come. Finally, we gave in. What we saw radically changed our lives. We fell in love with Argentina and felt an immediate affinity for the people. We were impressed by the effectiveness of the national Christians and what they were trying to accomplish. As we saw their needs, we felt an urgent, intense burden to help them. By the time we left, we had committed to building two housing complexes for married couples who wanted to come to the Bible Institute to study. The buildings were named *Dona Juana* and *Dona Sarah*.

From that time on, Joan and I knew what our role was to be: We were to use our entrepreneurial, managerial, and administrative abilities to generate funds—money that could be used to help others. We saw clearly that we could do more for the cause of missions by helping these nationals than by going ourselves. Our full-time ministry was to generate the funds needed to carry out the task of proclaiming the Good News about Christ. But where could we find a business that we could buy and build with the purpose of supporting missions?

When I returned from Argentina, I got a call from my accountant, Wendell Judd, asking me to take a consulting job with a direct selling jewelry company. I knew nothing about jewelry, but I did know a lot about the inner workings of a direct sales company, and Wendell knew from their books that they needed help. They were in serious trouble.

Joan and I went over to their offices and met with them. They had beautiful offices and surroundings, and forty thousand distributors on their rolls. I worked with them for several weeks, trying to help find a way to salvage their company. At one time they had done very well and professed to be a Christian company. I hated to see the company fold. As I looked at their operations, I began thinking—maybe this was a company we could buy and build. I knew direct sales and thought that jewelry would be a harmless enough product to sell.

I sent my attorney, Pat McManemin, to investigate the company with an eye to purchasing it. Every place he looked, he found more dishonesty and trouble. They did not practice what they preached. There were unpaid sales taxes, unpaid commissions, and only one-tenth of their sales force was actually working. They were forty thousand strong on paper, but only four thousand strong in the field. The company was a total disaster, and Pat counseled that under no circumstances should we purchase this company. They even offered to *give* it to us if we assumed their debt, but Pat said no. I was furious with him. My heart was set on acquiring this company. Why was he trying to block this perfect means of fulfilling the dream the Lord had given me? I knew that God wanted us involved. But the Bible does say that "in multitude of counselors there is safety" (Proverbs 24:6, KJV), so I listened. The Lord was working in my life because for once I didn't just bull my way forward. I followed Pat's truthful, wise counsel and reluctantly broke off all association with the company. It's a good thing I did. If I had not, there would be no Premier Designs because I would still be trying to untangle that company's royal mess! On the other hand, if I had not consulted with that company to begin with, there would be no Premier Designs because it was through this contact that the Lord opened the door into the direct selling jewelry industry.

The Premier Idea

Three or four months later, Gwen and Jack Mitchell, former executives of that now bankrupt jewelry company, called and asked if we had found a company yet. Obviously, they were out of work and were fishing in some new waters. Joan and I met with them, and this meeting triggered the idea of starting our own direct selling jewelry company.

I was not too excited about this possibility. When I left Home Interiors, I vowed never to be involved in a direct sales company again. I was burned out on it. Direct sales was at the bottom of my list of things God might lead us to do. (Being beach missionaries in Hawaii was at the top.) The reputation of many direct sales companies could compete with that of a crooked politician or a TV evangelist. Too many had not kept their promises, and many good people had been hurt. I did not want to be associated with this industry any more.

But then God gave me a vision. He didn't flash some bright sign in the skies over Dallas, nor did He come into my living room, sit down on the couch, and tell me what He wanted me to do. Instead, as I made intimacy with Him my top priority, as I daily allowed Him to talk to me through His Word, and as I talked to Him frequently in prayer, He gave me this solid feeling inside that He wanted me to start this company for Him. For two years, He had sent me on a reconnaissance tour of the needs on the mission field, and now He wanted me to do something about it. We were to start a company and make money to meet those needs.

Joan and I spent several weeks in prayer and discussions with our most trusted advisors. I met with some who questioned my desire and who told me that 1985 was not a good time to start a company, that direct sales were on the decline and there was too much uncertainty ahead. But we met with others who encouraged us. One particular incident stands out in my mind. Drs. Hazel and Howard Goddard, mature Christians and longtime friends and counselors, dropped by our house unexpectedly one evening. We spent the entire time talking about what Joan and I were considering—starting a company at age sixty! They listened carefully, asked wise questions, and then enthusiastically said, "Go for it!" (Ever since, Hazel, founder of Christian Counseling Ministries, has been one of our most trusted advisors, and Howard has been one of our faithful prayer partners and our Premier Designs chaplain.)

After much thought and prayer, we did decide to "go for it!" We would start a direct selling jewelry company built on a foundation of integrity and honesty, one whose most important asset would always be people. The profits would be shared with our employees, distributors, and ministries in America and around the world. Joan and I would fund the company and establish the philosophy, purpose, and way of doing business. The Mitchells would provide their experience in jewelry direct sales and run the company with us, with Jack appointed president, doing most of the work out in the field.

The Beginning

Premier was incorporated on November 5, 1985, in the upstairs office of our home on Red Cedar Trail in Dallas. We began operations on January 20, 1986, with six of us working: Joan, Jack, Gwen, Jack's secretary Pam, me, and my good friend and assistant from Home Interiors days, Bob Armstrong.

It was clear from the beginning that this company was to be "uniquely different." Our founding principles were *to honor God and serve others.* Our purpose was to *enrich every life we touched.* And perhaps most importantly of all, we were building the company on biblical principles. Our founding verse was Proverbs 16:11: "The Lord demands fairness in every business deal. He established this principle" (TLB). This was not just some high-sounding religious platitude. It meant that we needed to act with honesty and integrity in the real world of business and not make promises we could not keep. *The only thing we would promise was an opportunity.*

From day one, our four reasons for starting Premier were clearly stated:

1. We wanted a company that would support ministries around the world and in America.
2. We wanted to offer an opportunity for mothers to be able to stay home more with their children.
3. We wanted to minister to single parents and provide a way in which they could be encouraged, increase their self-esteem, and do something worthwhile while supporting their children.
4. We wanted a company that could provide a way for individuals, especially those in full-time Christian work, to meet their financial needs. At the same time, we wanted to provide an opportunity for wives of pastors and church staff members to find a ministry and identity of their own outside the church.

The more we got into the thinking and planning, the more excited we got. We could see that Premier was actually the culmination of forty years of experience. God was offering Joan and me an opportunity to put our beliefs and principles into practice, to help folks meet their financial needs, and to support His work around the world. The potential was awesome, and we could hardly wait to see all that God would do.

We held our first "Opportunity Presentation" in our home in December of 1985. Nita Barker, a friend and colleague from our Home Interiors days, signed up to become our very first "Jeweler," the name we gave our independent distributors. Bruce Peterson soon followed as a Jeweler and not too many months later began working with us to develop new markets. We were off and running. Within six months, we had three hundred people, and by the end of 1986, we had over seven hundred Jewelers in thirty-five states. The sky was as blue as a hot August day in Texas. But just as suddenly, thunderclouds began to gather on the horizon.

*"Find something you love to do
and would do for nothing; then find
someone who will pay you to do it."*

MARY CROWLEY

❧

*"People are always your road to success.
Love them enough to always
expect their best."*

ANDY HORNER

❧

CHAPTER EIGHT

The Rebirth of Premier

We were off to a great start. Premier Designs was growing. Joan and I were certain we were doing what God wanted us to do. Our philosophy and purpose were well thought out and written down. But in a matter of months it became clear that we had internal problems with our infant company. It had two completely different hearts, and it could not survive with this condition.

Times of Testing

From the beginning everyone in leadership had agreed to the same philosophy and purpose, but reports from the office and the field began to make it clear that this agreement was in word only. Some from the home office were not practicing what was being preached. Things were being done that contradicted everything we stood for.

Close friends warned us about the difficulties and advised Joan and me to increase our involvement. We had been overseeing the day-to-day operations, finances, and accounting, but had deliberately stayed in the background as far as the field operations went. Our friends warned that if we didn't get involved there, our financial investment could be lost. More importantly, Premier would lose its integrity, and thus its reason for being.

We heeded their counsel. Joan began paying all bills and watching the inventory and receiving. I ran the office, set up auditing practices, and developed more policies and procedures. We got involved in planning our rally and in some aspects of the training.

Even so, we continued to hear of things being said and promises being made that alarmed us. The emphasis was on making money, lots of it, and this emphasis contradicted everything we believed. The recruiting of new Jewelers was being placed ahead of serving others. "Book, sell, recruit"—and not necessarily in that order—was the motto. We were on the way to simply becoming another false-hope direct sales company more interested in profits than in people— exactly what Joan and I did not want.

Joan and I both remembered the exhaustion and hard work of going out into the field on a regular basis from our Home Interiors days, and in our sixties we hardly wanted to resume that pace again. But we also knew we must get to the field or the company's purpose would evaporate. We boarded planes and met the people, working to get the message across. But at this point, I made a big mistake. I let someone else remain as president and front the company, even though our difference in philosophy was apparent. I kept thinking that I could bring him around to my way of doing things and to my way of thinking. In the meantime, not many people realized that the company belonged to us or that the Horners were in control.

These early years were not only about power struggles and difficulties. There were also many blessings. Joan and

I continued to make mission trips, many with Bruce and Maggie, who shared our heart for missions. We got involved with an orphanage in Portugal and with Ireland Outreach. We extended our involvements through Word of Life ministries in Argentina, Bolivia, Brazil, Chile, Ecuador, Mexico, Paraguay, Poland, and Venezuela. God was opening our eyes to more and more needs, and the outreach of the company expanded. What a thrill to see God's plan unfold even though the developing storm in our office did not dissipate.

Peace in the Midst of Turmoil

Rushing through O'Hare airport in Chicago, I felt sharp chest pains. I had been noticing a growing fatigue, too—a kind of weariness and tiredness I hadn't experienced before. I must be getting old, I thought. Can't keep up the pace I used to! I wasn't sure what these symptoms meant, but I did decide to check things out. My cardiologist confirmed that I had some problems: three arteries were seriously blocked. He said that he thought they could "rotor rooter" the obstructions and I would be as good as new.

In November 1989 I underwent angioplasty surgery. It went well, and as I lay in the recovery room, a deep peace and a quiet joy came over me that I have never experienced before in my life. When I came out of that hospital, I emerged with a clear purpose. I would proclaim the truth regardless of what people thought. I would tell others what I believed and explain why God ordained this company. I would invest time in our leadership and make sure they "caught" the vision in their hearts, not just in their heads or with their mouths. Our company had been created to serve and to give hope to everyone we touched. We existed to influence the homes of America with service, hope, and joy. By God's grace and strength, this was going to become a reality.

As I recovered from surgery, I drafted my ideas in a document titled "Pathway through the '90s" that reiterated the philosophy and purpose of the company. I clearly set forth why the company was founded and what I envisioned for its future. I sketched out the creation of a Premier Foundation, which eventually would own part of the company and see to it that profits were distributed among various missions endeavors. I made it crystal clear that no one person would ever have ownership or control of Premier. I wasn't fooling around any more with any mixed purposes or ego trips.

This written clarification set in motion a coup within the ranks. I had tried for two years to conquer the divisiveness and conflict, to work with everyone, to give them time to come around. I had hoped that eventually we would be of one mind. That was not to be.

In response to the clear parameters of the "Pathway to the '90s" document, the president at the time secretly set up his own direct sales jewelry company in May 1990 and began to recruit our Jewelers. Rumors flew and things were said about us and about Premier that were absolutely untrue. People were told that Premier was going out of business, so they should jump ship while they could. Offers were made to our best people in an attempt to get them to leave and bring their downlines—the people they had sponsored into the business—with them. Joan and I were harassed, lied about, and called names, and this hurt us deeply. Even worse, people we cared about were being hurt, and that crushed us. By the time it was all over, nearly half our Jewelers went with them. It was a huge blow.

My lawyers wanted to fight: "Go get them, Andy! You have a solid case. We can destroy them!" My managers and field leadership counseled war: "You can't let them get away with this, Andy. They can't be allowed to do this!"

But something strange and unusual happened to me that had never happened before in my life. For once, I stayed quiet. What came to mind was the example of the most pure and honest man who ever lived as He stood before His accusers. He never said a word. I followed His example and vowed to love and forgive these people, rather than defend myself or fight them. And the silence proved to be more powerful than any words.

Premier: Phase Two

Despite the deep pain of that year, Joan and I can now look back and say that it was good. It was a time of needed purging. Our vision for Premier was purified and clarified. We recommitted ourselves to enriching lives, ministering to others, and serving. Those who weathered the storm with us were the cream of the crop, and we will always be grateful for their loyalty, support, and love during those difficult months. They were the ones who believed what we believed and had the same vision for Premier as we did. We were fewer in number, but we were stronger and more vital because everyone now had the same purpose. I always said that I would rather have ten people with heart and commitment than a thousand without it, and I believed that then more than ever.

Essentially, we had a brand new company and a brand new start. We had a strong foundation of committed people, and it was time to build. Joan and I spent the next several years on the road, encouraging our people, infusing them with hope and purpose, and communicating over and over again why Premier exists and what it is all about. We had never intended to be so involved or so busy when we started the company, but God had other plans, and as we obeyed, He blessed.

The company has grown and blossomed in a way we could never have planned or anticipated. You can see our first ten years of growth traced by the following graphs, which depict the annual increases in the number of active Jewelers, number of home shows, total retail sales, and net profits. By the end of 1995, we had over 6,000 Jewelers, who did more than 120,000 home shows and retailed over 60 million dollars for the year. We purchased our 56,000 square foot headquarters building that is on twelve acres of land in Las Colinas in 1992, and developed a five-year plan to expand our space to over 110,000 square feet. We now have 150 home office employees working in that building. In addition, in 1992, we acquired a 38-acre site north of Dallas that we call "Haven of Hope." We use this facility for trainings, meetings, and retreats, and have plans to continue expanding it in the future to accommodate our needs.

These are the facts and the history of the birth of Premier. But what about the inner workings? What makes the company tick? What is the heart of Premier and what are the principles that continue to guide it? Why is Premier a company people trust?

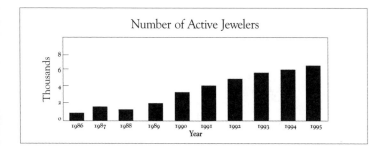

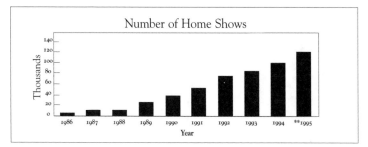

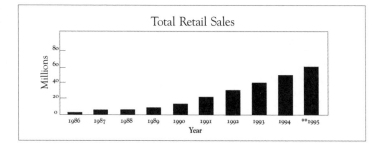

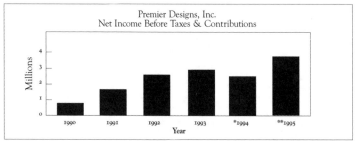

* 1994 incurred many one-time expenditures related to building remodeling, staff additions and new computer system implementation.
**1995 income estimated

PART TWO

The Heart of Premier

*"It is important how you view your business.
If you look at serving, instead of selling,
you will be richly rewarded."*

ANDY HORNER

❧

*"Forget about the sales you hope to make.
Concentrate on the service
you want to render."*

HARRY BULLIS;
FORMER CEO OF GENERAL MILLS

❧

CHAPTER NINE

The Inverted Pyramid

*T*he black stretch limousine pulls up to the curb in New York City. The windows are tinted and everything about the car whispers wealth and power. The chauffeur rushes to open the door for his passenger. As Donald Trump strides into his Trump Towers, a battery of secretaries, managers, and personal aides jumps to meet his every need. This is the epitome of business success—to reach the apex of the pyramid, the top, where everyone now serves you.

In 3000 B.C. the Pharaohs mobilized an entire nation to build the pyramids to ensure that their names would be remembered forever. As we enter A.D. 2000, the Pharaohs of modern business build their skyscrapers and mobilize their armies of employees to meet their ego needs. Having others wait on you hand and foot—isn't this what being at the top is all about?

Top Down Pyramid

The organizational diagram of a hierarchical, top-down corporation would look something like this:

This type of organization is typical of today's corporations. The customers provide the foundation of the entire structure, supporting each of the subsequent levels. Employees are there to support the managers and all those above them, and managers are there to support the CEO and his executives. Those at the very top of the company don't have to worry about supporting anyone. They have reached the zenith of power where they can do what they want, as long as they make sure that the company keeps making money.

The Pyramid Turned Upside Down

In contrast to most business tycoons who don Armani suits and monogrammed silk shirts, the most powerful man who ever lived took off His robe, wrapped a towel around His waist, and proceeded to wash the filthy, smelly feet of His disciples. He taught us that true success is not climbing up, but bowing down to meet the needs of others. He said, "The first shall be last and the last shall be first."

Following His example, we do things a little different-ly at Premier Designs. Our organizational chart is upside down when compared to most. I call it the "Inverted Pyramid." It was never taught to me in college, nor had I ever heard of it in my years of corporate experience.

As you can see, the difference between this pyramid and the more typical top-down pyramid on the previous

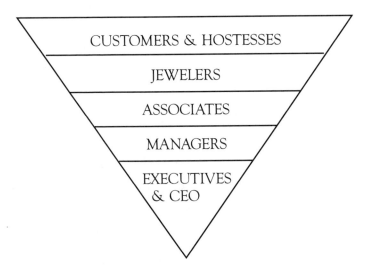

CUSTOMERS & HOSTESSES

JEWELERS

ASSOCIATES

MANAGERS

EXECUTIVES
& CEO

page is that the "higher" you go in this upside down orga-nizational structure, the more people you are responsible to support and serve. Those who purchase the jewelry (the customers) and those who provide a home in which the Jewelers present the jewelry (the hostesses) are at the top of the pyramid. The people who sell the jewelry (Jewelers), Associates, and other managers follow. Those in "higher" positions don't have more people serving them; they have more people to serve. This demonstrates what I believe is a fundamental truth: *Leading is serving and serving is lead-ing.* Advancement means greater responsibility in meeting the needs of others; it means becoming a servant. Do you want to move up the ladder? Learn to support others and meet their needs. Want a title and more responsibility? Become a better servant.

Looking at our pyramid, you might say, "That's top heavy. It looks like it could topple over any minute, with just the slightest nudge." It won't. It is held firmly in position by four strong pillars: our philosophy, our purpose, our plan, and our service.

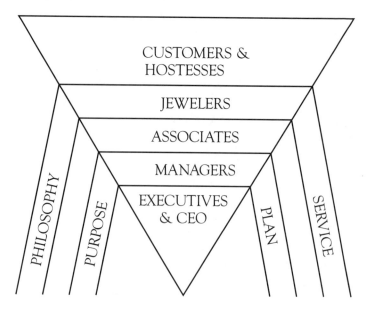

Our Philosophy

We believe that every person has worth and value because they are created by God and in His image. Mary Crowley repeatedly reminded me, "God did not take time to make a nobody." We believe that God created every person with value and that every person deserves our respect. We believe that people are important not because of what they achieve, but because of who they are. We believe that people are our most important asset.

We believe in America and the free enterprise system. We love this country and the freedom and opportunity we have to achieve in direct proportion to our willingness to work.

We believe that it is more important to build a successful life than a successful business. Real success comes when your priorities are in the right place and your life is in balance: *God first, family second, work third.*

Our Purpose

We clearly stated our purpose in November 1985 when we began Premier, and it is still the same: *To Enrich Every Life We Touch.* This means that we must *serve, share,* and *care,* striving to add something positive to each life that we come in contact with. As a company, enriching lives means *providing a way for those who join the Premier family to find identity, achievement, and success, and to meet their personal and financial needs.* Everyone that God has created has the basic need to feel that they are valued, that they belong, and that they are competent. As a company, Premier reassures people of their worth and value. It provides a family for them to belong to and helps them succeed in their business.

As individuals, this means that we serve, expecting nothing in return; we give without getting. We care, whether or not that person is nice, whether or not she buys a single piece of jewelry, and even if she cancels her home show or no one comes. In fact, some of the best home shows are the ones where no guests show up. In that situation, the Jeweler has a special opportunity to reach out and encourage that hostess, to get to know her and discover what her needs are, to bring some special caring into that home. As Oswald Chambers writes, "One way to measure a person's character is to observe the way he or she treats people who cannot possibly do them any good." That is the kind of selfless giving we aim for.

Our Plan

Retailing through home shows is our plan, and we have an excellent hostess plan (we believe one of the best you will find anywhere) that motivates and generously rewards the hostess for holding a home show. We could sell our jewelry through stores, catalogs, a shopping channel, or even the Internet, but our experience has shown that home shows are the most effective means.

First of all, home shows are the best way to fulfill our purpose of enriching lives. They allow us into the homes of America to bring a dose of hope. Because they provide an opportunity to build long-term relationships and give personalized service to hostesses and customers, home shows allow Jewelers to demonstrate their caring and to practice what we preach.

Additionally, home shows are the most direct way for our Jewelers to grow their businesses and achieve immediate financial rewards. Jewelers receive their profit as soon as they make the sale, that very night, resulting in immediate income. Moreover, building relationships with hostesses and customers through home shows creates a retail base and a pool of people who will be repeat hostesses and customers. We have some hostesses who not only become their Jeweler's friend, but also enthusiastically hold four or five shows a year. And if the Jeweler is interested in building a sales organization, experience has shown that she will find her best sponsoring contacts at home shows.

Service

Serving others is the heart of Premier. I cannot emphasize this enough. The company is saturated with a focus on service. When you call our home office, the phone is answered, "How may I serve you?" We talk about service constantly, train on it, write about it, and even paint it on our walls. We have it on our letterhead: "Serving with care since 1985." Jewelers are trained to serve customers; our home office employee Associates (employees) are trained to serve and support our Jewelers; and we all try to serve and help one another in whatever ways we can. All of our people understand that service is the road to success. Everything we do relates to service.

All this talk about service could sound saccharine and unrealistic, and we certainly are not perfect at it, but let me assure you that this is not just talk. Serving others is not just a slogan or some program we do halfheartedly. We mean it. If you come by our home office, I believe you will feel it. You will sense a difference because this attitude of serving is deep in the heart of our Associates. We work diligently and tirelessly to create and maintain this service atmosphere at our home office and to communicate this attitude to everyone who comes into the Premier family.

We do the same with our Jewelers in the field. As Joan and I travel the country, meeting and talking with our Jewelers, we constantly talk about service. Over and over, we repeat our message that serving others is the road to success and fulfillment. We say it again and again, and then we say it some more because we want people to get this from their heads into their hearts. We want them to understand that true service is an attitude that sincerely asks of every situation, "How can I turn this into an opportunity to serve?"

For example, we sell jewelry, the number one gift item in America. Jewelry is a great product and we are very proud of our line, but it is also a delicate, vulnerable product. Jewelry can break, stones can fall out, and finishes can tarnish. Because of these problems, it can be a frustrating product at times. What I want our Jewelers to see is that these problems are, in fact, opportunities to serve. Instead of looking at these situations as time-wasters and impediments to their businesses, those with true serving hearts will see these situations as exciting opportunities to serve their customers and go out of their way to help, expecting nothing back.

A Lesson from Napoleon

In my house I have a small collection of Napoleon ceramics. Why? It is said of Napoleon that he was a gifted man, a visionary, and a dreamer of dreams. His leadership in war was excelled by none. When he overthrew the royalty, he had good intentions. He wanted to help and improve the living conditions in the lives of the common people. Considered a brilliant leader, Napoleon is remembered for quotes such as, "Courage is like love. It must have hope for nourishment," and "I would rather have one lion lead a hundred antelopes than a hundred antelopes lead one lion." He understood the meaning of leadership and had great success, as history reveals.

But Napoleon was unable to handle his successes and wanted more. Conquering most of Europe was not enough. He wanted to conquer the world. As he lost his original purpose, selfishness, recognition, and power corrupted him. He was a dynamic young man, but ended up an old man in despair, a prisoner on the isle of Corsica. I have a picture of Napoleon in his early days, young and handsome. And I have a picture of him in his later days, an old man, hopeless and broken.

Years have passed and times have changed since the days of Napoleon. However, human nature has not changed. People start out with a purpose to help and serve others. But often when they receive recognition, they are corrupted by power and decide enough is never enough. The grace with which a leader handles success has a tremendous influence on others. As Albert Schweitzer said, "Example is not the main thing in influencing others, it is the only thing." This is why it is so important that the leaders of a company maintain the desire and ability to serve others, even as the company reaches greater success.

All of this idealistic emphasis on service and caring for others will mean nothing if it is not combined with solid management principles. I've had over forty years of hands-on experience in the world of big business and in the Home Interiors world of direct sales. Let me share some of the practical principles I have gleaned from this experience.

ly at age two in
ʼast, Ireland.

Joan's baby picture - born in
Woodstock, Ontario, Canada.

Above: *Andy's boyhood home on Upper Charleville Street, Belfast, Ireland.*
Left: *Andy's mother, Sarah, in Woodstock, Ontario, shortly before her death in 1947.*

Above: *Andy's mother's grave site in Woodstock, Ontario. The inscription on the headstone reads, "It is no vain thing to wait upon the Lord."*
Left: *Bill and Mary Blair and their children. The Blairs were the first people Andy and Joan met when they arrived in Dallas in 1950. The Blairs helped Andy find a job. They became life-long friends and the "Horner's" best cheerleaders.*

ʌve: Andy at age four with
mother, Sarah, in Belfast,
ʌnd.

Left: *Andy with his brothers (L-R) Hugh, Andy, Sam, Tommy, Bill, and his sister, Chris (Third from left) are shown here in 1982 at a Horner Family Reunion at Barrington College, R.I. Andy was one of thirteen brothers and sisters.*

The "Duchess of Richmond" the ship that brought Andy and his family to Canada in 1931.

Above: *Andy at age 13 standi with fellow workers at the Ma Dairy in Woodstock, Ontario, where Andy worked as a bottl washer.*
Top Inset: *The apartment abo the Maple Dairy where Andy his family lived for 15 years i Woodstock, Ontario.*

Andy (Center) and his fellow hockey team members in 1934.

Andy and the Woodstock Y.M.C.A. basketball team in 1940.

Above: *Andy with the 1934 Ford he an his mother used for their janitorial bus ness. This car also won Andy a lot of friends in Woodstock including Joan.*
Left: *The Woodstock Railway Station where Andy met the train and picked u the Toronto Star newspaper each day delivery.*

ove: Andy and Joan as
nagers in Woodstock.
ght: Joan's high school
arbook picture.

ove: Andy and Joan's
dding on March 9, 1946.
ght: New St. Paul's
urch in Woodstock, the
urch in which they were
rried.

ght Bottom: Andy and
n's first new car, a 1952
dge. Andy jokes that this
r cost him about $40,000
cause he refinanced it so
ny times! Andrea is also
own here as a child.

**Top Right
Corner:**
Sig. Horner in
his Canadian
Sailor uniform
in 1943.
Above: Andy
and Joan stand-
ing in front of
their first apart-
ment in
Woodstock,
Ontario, in
1946.

Right: *The first home Andy and Joan owned in Dallas in 1954.*

Left: *Andy and Joan's home, today, in Dallas.*

Andy and Joan's children in Racine, Wisconsin in 1961. (L-R) Mary, Tim, Tommy, Andrea, and Sarah.

Above Standing: *(L-R) Tim Horner, Andrea Horner, Tommy Horner* **Seated:** *(L-R) Sarah Horner Wetzel, Andy and Joan, and Mary Horner Collins*

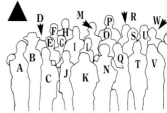

Above: *Andy's 75th Birthday was celebra[ted] in Ireland in July of 1999; A. Kathryn Horner, B. Andy, C. Drew Horner, D. An[drea] Horner, E. Donna Horner, F. Eric Billigmeier, G. Tommy Horner, H. Alex Figert, I. Erin Figert, J. Justin Horner, K. Tim Horner, L. Jolie Horner, M. Laur[a] Collins, N. Joan, O. Caris Wetzel, P. Tho[mas] Horner, Q. McKenzie Horner, R. Miah Wetzel, S. Sarah Wetzel, T. Jessica Horne[r], U. Jack Collins, V. Gabrielle Wetzel, W. M[?] Collins, X. Jake Wetzel, Y. Johannah Wet[zel]*

Right: *Andy and Joan with all their grand children; A. Erin Billigmeier, B. Justin Horner, C. McKenzie Horner, D. Kathryn Horner, E. Thomas Horner, F. Miah Wetzel, G. Jessica Horner, H. Joan Horner, I. Eric Billigmeier, J. Andy Horner, K. JolieAnn Horner, L. Drew Horner, M. Caris Wetzel, N. Johannah Wetzel, O. Gabey Wetzel*

Below: Criswell College in Dallas. Andy has been involved in Criswell College since its founding in 1970.

ve: Andy with faculty of Criswell ege on the occasion of Andy receiving honorary Doctorate on May 11, 1986.

y and Joan with their Bible Study class, the mblelites."

ove: Andy, Joan, d Dr. Criswell in 91 at the dedica-n of Horner Hall Criswell College.
ove Right: dy and Joan at dedication of Sarah Horner hearsal Hall in 78 at First ptist Church in llas in honor of dy's mother, rah.

Above: Andy's precious inheritance, his mother's Bible.
Below: Joan and her Christian friend, Marie Hunter in Dallas.

Left: Hazel and Howard Goddard, life long friends, counselors, and prayer partners.

Left: *Andy (Far Left) a the Johnson Wax leade ship in Racine, Wiscon in 1961.*
Below: *Andy (Bottom Left) and the Xerox ma agement in 1966.*

Above: *Joan, Mary Crowley (mentor, dear friend, and Founder of Home Interiors) and Andy.*
Left: *Andy, Mary Crowley, and Don Carter in August of 1972 on the occa sion of Andy's promotion to Vice President of Administration for Home Interiors.*

Right: *Randy Draper, Andy, Tom Landry, Bob Thompson, and Greg Terrell at the Tom Landry Fellowship of Christian Athletes Golf Tournament in 1994.*

Left: Andy and the orphans of the Lar Evangélico orphanage in Portugal in 1987, a ministry dear to Andy and Joan's heart.

Below: Andy and Joan at Premier's Home Office in Dallas in front of the display of 31 flags which represent the countries around the world in which Premier has the opportunity to share in ministries.

ve: Andy (Far Right) and the Mission
ctors of Word of Life in South
erica. The Word of Life ministry world-
e is a favorite of Andy and Joan's
use of its far reaching ministry and its
ctice of training nationals to be mis-
aries in their own countries and
nd the world.
ht: Sophie Mueller with Joan in
ezuela. Sophie spent 50 years of her
in the jungles of Venezuela and
umbia translating the Bible and teach-
the Word. Premier built a Bible
itute in Venezuela in 1993.

Left: Joan and the residents of the Dona Juana (named after Joan) efficiency apartments for married students of the Word of Life Institute in Argentina.

(L) Randy and Elizabeth Draper and (R) Melissa and Greg Terrell are shown here with Joan and Andy Horner (Center) at the dedication of the new Home Office building on Corporate Drive in Las Colinas (Irving, Texas).

Andy and Joan by the fountain that adorns the front of Premier's Home O~~~ in Dallas. The fountain was given to A~~ on the occasion of his 70th Birthday ~~ August of 1994. The inscription reads, "~ among you as one who serves" —Luke 22.~

Above: Premier's Home Office Management Team: (Top L–R) Jeff DiMiceli, Leonard Fisher, Don Barker, Andrea Horner, Kevin Moses, Ed Creek, Lynn Hobson (Bottom L-R) Kenneth Hays, Woody Marr, James Johnson, Gary Golden, Elbert Johnson.

Insets Above: Premier's first offices at 3150 Premier Drive in 1986 and Premier's next off~ at 3100 Premier Drive in 1989 both in Las Colinas (Irving, Texas).
Left and Below: Premier's new corporate offic~ at 1551 Corporate Drive also in Las Colinas (Irving, Texas) on 12 acres purchased in 1993~

> *"For the Lord grants wisdom! His every word is a treasure of knowledge and understanding…He shows how to distinguish right from wrong, how to find the right decision every time."*

PROVERBS 2:6, 9

⚜

> *"After a company is established, service and support are the keys to success."*

ANDY HORNER

CHAPTER TEN

Management Principles

*A*t Premier Designs, we operate with skilled managers who utilize proven management practices. This is a well-run company, and our operations and accounting practices stand up to the toughest scrutiny. I brought to Premier almost twenty years of experience in corporate America and eighteen years of experience in direct selling. From these years of work, I gleaned a set of business principles and management activities that have guided Premier from the beginning. They make us *uniquely different* from any other direct selling company that I know of.

These distinctive principles are significant for two reasons. First, *they work.* Premier is a successful and growing company that continues to demonstrate the truth and power of these principles. Second, I want to dispel the notion that there is some inherent contradiction between building a company on biblical principles and managing a company with sound financial and business principles. In my mind, they are one and the same thing.

It's easy for a business person to put on his or her fancy clothes on Sunday morning and sing the hymns with gusto. It's another thing to bring God into the Monday morning world of buying and selling. I believe honoring God gets down to the basics. It means you are truthful, honest, and financially responsible. It means you never make promises you cannot keep. It means you use the mind God gave you. Solid business principles, whether you claim to be a Christian or not, are essential to building a solid company. We pay the consequences in life and in business for foolish decisions and mismanagement.

Principle #1: Put People First

I firmly believe that people are the most important asset any company has. This means *people come first at Premier*. We focus on people—our customers, our hostesses, our Jewelers, and our home office Associates—rather than on profit, production, or product. Remember our emphasis on serving? This means that meeting the needs of people is a higher priority than selling jewelry.

I prefer to call Premier a *direct service* company, rather than a direct sales company. I make this distinction because there is a difference between a company that emphasizes sales, production, and the bottom line, and a company that puts people first, supporting them and serving them, expecting nothing in return. Our Jewelers are never asked, "How were your sales this month?" We have no nationally sponsored sales meetings, no weekly or monthly sales reports, and no quotas. We believe and train that success comes in serving others and seeing lives changed, not in selling jewelry. Our focus is people.

Although Premier is primarily about people and not profits, this does not mean that there isn't opportunity to make a good profit. We have seen time and time again that *you can sell without serving, but you cannot serve without sell-*

ing. Most people sign up to make money and many do very well. We want them to do well. We offer one of the best money-making opportunities available. However, we also want them to think beyond the money to serving people.

People First in the Field

Joan and I decided when we started Premier that our focus was not going to be on making big money for the company or enriching ourselves financially. The company would have to make enough of a profit to stay in business, of course, but beyond that, we wanted the people who do the work to make the money. Mary Crowley taught us well. "Andy," she would say, "you find enough people to care about, and *you help them succeed*, and you can't help but succeed yourself."

We knew the wisdom of her words and put them into practice. We instituted a higher than normal pay out on sales—50 percent—almost unheard of in the direct sales industry, along with a very generous commission structure of 10 percent three levels down, plus extra percentages for moving up in our Diamond Designer leadership program. We certainly could have structured this differently and less generously, but we knew that if we meant what we said—that people were first—this meant that they must be first in the pay out. Their earnings needed to be generous enough that doing home shows and building a business was well worth their time and efforts and would provide them an opportunity for financial success in direct proportion to the time and work that they invested.

In addition to providing the opportunity for good incomes, we wanted to do everything we could to help the Jewelers succeed at their businesses. To this day, we keep our jewelry prices as low as possible so Jewelers can sell it more easily, even if it means our profit margins are small-er. We mark up our business supplies and catalogs very lit-tle, if any, so a Jeweler's cost of doing business stays as low as possible. We pay for all shipping and postage, even though those costs routinely exceed the small annual licensing fee the Jewelers pay. We do no advertising. Instead, we put the money back into the Jewelers' busi-nesses with promotions, contests, incentives, and subsi-dies—all aimed at helping the Jeweler succeed. In other words, *we put our money where our Jewelers are.*

Not only does the principle of *people first* guide our financial decisions, it also influences our thinking when we develop policies and procedures. Joan and I felt that putting our people first meant that we should go the extra mile for them in terms of our home office support and ser-vice. We determined to do everything we could to make their businesses as hassle-free as possible.

For example, we fill orders by customer and by home show, and then package them accordingly so that the Jeweler has no unpacking, dividing up, and repackaging to do. We didn't want them receiving large boxes of mer-chandise for several home shows at a time, requiring them to spend a lot of time processing their customer orders. Moreover, we file sales taxes for all our Jewelers, regardless of where they live. We provide monthly activity reports for each Jeweler, keeping track of all purchases, sales, and commissions. All this is included in the reasonable annu-al renewal fee and keeps the business as simple as possi-ble. Although these services translate into higher operating costs for the home office and distribution cen-ter, they give our Jewelers more time to focus on people, which is where we want their focus to be.

Our focus on people extends to our programs of awards and recognitions as well. It is typical in direct sales companies that those who achieve and sell the most are the ones who are recognized and honored, and they should be. We recognize our top performers with awards and prizes, onstage presentations at our rallies, pins, and certificates. However, we also wanted to honor those who do such an awesome job and work so hard but who, because of circumstances or personality or timing, will never be top achievers. We wanted ways to recognize people for *who they are, not just what they do.*

Over the years we have inaugurated a number of awards for those who embody the heart and vision of Premier, the caring and sharing principles that guide us. For example, we instituted our Princess royalty program, Mr. Premier, and Precious Gems program for those from the field who personify consistent and genuine serving and caring. We select Associates of the Year from the office and distribution center, recognizing them for their competence, but mainly for their attitude of serving others. Recently, we inaugurated our annual Servant's Heart Award for that individual within our organization, in the home office or the field, who best exemplifies the Premier spirit of service. At Premier, these awards for "who you are" are the highest awards you can receive.

People First in the Home Office

Most of the examples I have given relate to ways that we put people first out in the field. However, our policies and practices in the home office distribution center also focus on people. We realize the essential contribution that everyone in the home office makes to the success of our company. Every job that is done is important, and every person makes a valuable contribution. We take every opportunity we can to express our appreciation, both in words and in actions. In fact, we decided that the term *employee* didn't really reflect the reality of our company. Rather, we are "Associates," all working together in an enterprise we believe in. Without our Associates, we wouldn't be where we are today.

Focusing on people in the home office means that we want our Associates to receive fair wages and to share the profits of the company. We take care of our Associates before we do anything else. We have profit sharing programs, 401(k)'s, a generous benefit package, a loan program, a school reimbursement plan, and a scholarship program for college students. We host our annual Christmas party, Associates' banquet, and fall family company picnic where we give bonuses, gifts, prizes, and cash. We have counseling services available to all our Associates, ranging from one-time visits to intensive week-long stays for in-depth counseling. And my door is never shut. I am available and eager to meet with any of our people who need or want to talk. They come first.

The principle of putting people first at the home office even influenced the decision about the location of our new corporate headquarters. When we decided to buy our new building in 1992, there were many buildings for sale in the Dallas area. We could have done better price-wise and helped out our bottom line if we had moved farther east than we did. However, most of our people live west of our office. Joan and I decided that if our people truly come first, they should be a more important factor in where we located the company than the financial implications. We bought west.

I imagine that some of you think we must be nuts to make decisions this way. But I want to tell you that there is power in this principle of putting people first. Sure, it may have reduced our profits somewhat, but I believe that you never give without getting even more back. How do you measure in dollars the value of employee loyalty, happiness in their job and with their workplace, high morale, and the extra efforts that are made because they know they are truly cared about and appreciated? I remember Mary Crowley's coaching, "Andy, you build the people and the people will build the business." She was right.

People First with Our Suppliers

Our principle of putting people first also extends to our suppliers and vendors. We are grateful for their products and services. We need the boxes and paper, the equipment and phone lines, and good quality jewelry. One of the first things Joan and I did back in 1990, after the company's realignment, was to visit our jewelry suppliers in Rhode Island. We deliberately went to see each one at their plants. We wanted to get to know them personally and see their businesses and how they operated. It was a valuable time of bridge building and we developed relationships that we treasure to this day.

In 1993, we gave an appreciation dinner for our Rhode Island suppliers. We thanked them for their good service, told them about our business philosophy, and let them know that we considered them a vital part of our Premier team. These folks meant more to us than just a source of product. What a strange experience for these battle-hardened business people! They weren't used to being cared about personally. They were used to being manipulated and pitted against one another. Their enthusiastic response became one more proof of the importance of our first and foremost principle of doing business—focus on people.

The Personal Touch

We believe that putting people first also requires a personal touch. When you call Premier, a person will answer the phone. We do not have automated answering that presents some complicated menu in order for you to direct your call. Automated answering and voice mail are absolutely forbidden! We have real live operators, an anachronism in this day and age. It is people to people, not people to machine or system. It would be a lot cheaper to have automated answering—paying three or four operators to answer phones and direct calls is expensive—but I believe personal service is vital if we are to be a company whose central focus is truly people. We cannot lose that personal touch.

Now don't get me wrong. Technology can be good, and we use every bit available to help us do a better job of serving people. We use very sophisticated hardware and software systems for order processing, inventory control, accounting, and shipping. We are committed to staying abreast of all new developments and upgrading as we need to, even though sometimes it seems we are upgrading daily! But our computers and systems do not dictate what we do. They are tools to be used to better serve our people, but never, never, never are they substitutes for a person!

Sometimes maintaining a personal touch takes extra effort, but it is always worth it. It lets people know how much you care about them and appreciate them. Joan and I write personal notes to our folks in the field and in the home office distribution center. Joan even hand writes every one of hers. We do not have form letters that we send out or people to answer our mail for us. We stay in touch, person-to-person, and it means so much. I personally sign all commission checks over five hundred dollars and all management checks. This takes two or three days out of my month, but I wouldn't do it any other way. It gives me an opportunity to add a note of encouragement and thanks. For me focusing on people means that our contacts with people must be this personal. People will always come first at Premier.

Principle #2: Control the Growth

Over the years, I have seen too many direct sales companies grow faster than they were able to support and collapse in on themselves. When the demands of the field outrun the ability of the home office to supply and service, the company is dead.

We decided that in order to avoid these problems we would deliberately control our growth. We wanted Premier to grow very slowly and carefully. We were not interested in big numbers. Instead, we would invest in a smaller number of people. We would train them and help them really work their businesses. If they followed the home show plan, with an emphasis on retailing rather than recruiting, we knew that both they and the company would be building on strong foundations.

Controlling growth also meant that we would not finance Premier's expanding operations by going into debt. We determined that the company would grow at a rate that it could sustain financially by itself, not with borrowed money. Although we realized that the day might come when some debt was necessary, we did not want to go out on any financial limbs simply for the purpose of getting big.

If we wanted to get big fast, we certainly could. We know how to do it. You simply require a very small investment to get started and offer incentives for joining that are too good to refuse. Then you watch the numbers grow. Getting big is not difficult, but it can be a problem.

In May 1995, we celebrated Joan's birthday with twelve days of special home show bonuses and incentives given to new Jewelers who signed up. Within a day or two, we were swamped with orders and new contracts. Within three days we were a week behind, within five days we were two weeks behind, and by the end of the contest we had things so piled up we were three to four weeks behind. Things were out of control quickly, and there was much frustration and unhappiness in the field. Customers waited two or three weeks to get orders that are usually filled in three days. All this was a vivid reminder: control the growth! Premier is not about getting big; it is about enriching lives and serving others. It is about being sure we can adequately train, serve, and support the Jewelers who sign on.

Tight control of finances is as important as tight control of growth. We are conservative in all of our financial operations. Since day one, we have taken extra efforts never to commingle monies. We never spend the money we collect for sales taxes. That money goes directly into an escrow account and is kept completely separate from our operating capital. We never spend commission money. The earned commissions are put aside in escrow until the commission checks are issued.

In addition, beginning in our first year of operation, we have had outside auditors come in semiannually to check everything over. We never want anything done that is not completely in line with standard accounting practices, the law, and business ethics. We are proud to be members of the Direct Selling Association (DSA), an organization made up of direct selling companies who have been carefully checked out over a one-year period and who meet the high ethical and legal standards of the group. There are many wonderful direct selling companies who are members, and we are happy to be associated with them. Likewise, we applaud and support the efforts of the DSA in rooting out non-compliant and unethical direct sales companies and raising the standards of the industry as a whole.

In summary, we are conservative, risk aversive, and debt avoidant in our financial operations. We pay all our vendors on time and have never been even a day late with paychecks and commission checks. Our growth is slow and controlled, so that we can provide the service and support to the field that are essential to sustain the company over the long term. We do not grow any faster than we can serve. The principle of controlled growth and responsible finances permeates everything we do in the home office and out in the field. This is one message I preach loud and clear!

Principle #3: Commit to a Shared Vision

When I began to think about starting a direct sales company at the age of sixty, I had a clear vision of what kind of company I wanted it to be: a company where serving and caring were the objectives above all others. This is the vision that motivates and inspires Joan and me and most of those who join Premier Designs. People need to make money, and they can in Premier, but what our people get the most excited about and motivated by is this added dimension of their business: that their work has meaning and purpose beyond just the money.

Communicating this vision for Premier with all who join us is a major part of my role at Premier. I feel it is my responsibility to keep these guiding principles in front of our Associates and Jewelers alike. I want our Associates to understand the scope of what they do. They are not just inspecting a piece of jewelry; they also are helping a Jeweler serve her customer better. They are not just entering an order or packing a box; they are helping a Jeweler build a successful life and business. I want them to see the purpose and the meaning of everything they do, no matter how mundane it may seem. People find more energy and enjoyment in their work when they see that they are part of a much bigger picture.

What keeps a Jeweler going who has just had her tenth home show cancellation or postponement? Or what keeps a Jeweler going who has achieved all of her financial goals? It is the vision of serving and caring that she shares with the other Jewelers in her Premier family and with the Associates in the home office. She is part of a bigger purpose.

When we need to hire personnel for the home office, part of the interviewing process, of course, is telling the applicant what the purpose of our company is all about. If I talk to them personally, that is all I talk about. I don't talk about job title or job descriptions, resumes or opportunities for advancement. Instead, I talk about our shared commitment to serving others. If they don't get excited about that, then Premier is probably not the place for them. We want employees with a heartfelt commitment to this way of doing business.

Unlike most direct sales companies, we do not hire our field leadership from the outside. All of our leadership starts off the same way—carrying a sample jewelry kit. All of our leaders walk the road of experience and understand the reason we exist. They share our philosophy that serving and caring bring rich blessings and total fulfillment, and they have experienced it for themselves. Developing our own leadership from within is essential if we are to maintain a company-wide commitment to our vision of serving and caring.

When a Jeweler invites someone to join Premier, this same commitment is necessary. Our Jewelers sponsor people one at a time. When they invite someone into this business, we insist that they nurture them, encourage them, and work with them. They must spend the personal time necessary to train them and infuse them with our philosophy, purpose, and guiding principles. We believe that it is our commitment to this shared vision that keeps us strong.

Principle #4: Continue to Improve

At Premier, we welcome complaints! Compliments are nice and we are happy to get them. We all like to hear when we are doing a good job and when we have made a difference to someone. However, we don't learn how to improve when everything is going smoothly. We learn how to improve from problems. I have found that we get some of our best ideas about how we can improve our service, our product, and our procedures from dissatisfied people who had the courage to say so. A problem is an opportunity to improve.

Premier is far from perfect. We have many areas where we could do better. That's not to say that we are doing a bad job or that we are a poorly run company, because we're not. It is just to emphasize that we are always on the lookout for ways to improve.

For example, we are constantly looking for ways to improve our customer service. We decided one way to do this would be to give our Jewelers better access to our customer service. So we gave toll-free phone numbers to all the major departments related to serving our people more effectively. Our hope is that this will result in more personalized service.

Additionally, our Jewelers brought to our attention ways in which the use of their personal computers would simplify their paperwork and ordering process. After much research, we instituted an on-line ordering program and have participated in the development of order software. I could give many more examples, but the point is that such changes are all guided by one principle: our commitment to finding ways to improve.

In summary, we have four guiding business principles at Premier Designs that affect our decision-making, our policies, our planning, and our operations. We ask ourselves these questions: *Are we putting people first? Does this reflect careful financial planning and does it promote slow, controlled growth? Are we advancing the company's commitment to a shared vision of serving and caring? Is there some way we could do this better?* In order for these guiding principles to guide us day by day at Premier there are also some management activities that must be implemented. I call this our POSDA Plan.

1987 Verse of the Year

"Love is very patient and kind, never jealous or envious, never boastful or proud, never haughty or selfish or rude. Love does not demand its own way. It is not irritable or touchy. It does not hold grudges and will hardly even notice when others do it wrong. It is never glad about injustice, but rejoices whenever truth wins out. If you love someone you will be loyal to him no matter what the cost. You will always believe in him, always expect the best of him, and always stand your ground in defending him."

1 CORINTHIANS 13:4-7 TLB

⚜

1988 Verse of the Year

"And now this word to all of you: You should be like one big happy family, full of sympathy toward each other, loving one another with tender hearts and humble minds. Don't repay evil for evil. Don't snap back at those who say unkind things about you. Instead, pray for God's help for them, for we are to be kind to others, and God will bless us for it."

1 PETER 3:8-9 TLB

⚜

....

CHAPTER ELEVEN

Management Activities

*B*eyond the principles that guide day-to-day business at Premier Designs, there are also management activities that are crucial to the effective implementation of these principles. I refer to this management strategy as *POSDA*.

<u>P</u>lan

I believe in prayer, and we do pray at Premier Designs. Not only do we pray as managers at the home office, but we also have committed prayer partners all around the world praying for every aspect of our company and its operations. However, as much as we pray, we plan more. I believe there is a time when God makes clear our responsibility and we must think and then act.

Planning is an important function for us. It is our road map to the future. We plan for the short term and the long term, for the home office distribution center and the field.

We have plans for five years from now, as well as plans for this week, this month, and this year. Our business plans encompass all aspects of our operations, from anticipating building and physical plant needs to forecasting leadership and training needs. We plan financially with a yearly budget that is reviewed every six months and with daily and weekly appraisals of cash flow. We plan so we can control our growth, avoid debt, and make sure that we have—and will have everything in place to be able to service and support our Jewelers.

Organize

Obviously, a well-organized operation is more efficient and effective than one that is in a continuous state of chaos. Therefore, it is always worth the effort to get things organized and running smoothly. At Premier, we organize around the principle of serving our Jewelers. Home office departments are structured according to the areas of service that we provide. In fact, every department's name has "services" in it, and every manager oversees some area of "service," such as Financial Services, Jeweler and Customer Services, or Marketing Services.

Our procedures and staffing are determined by what will serve our people best. For example, we have organized and staffed our home show processing and order filling operations to achieve the shortest time cycle possible for the Jeweler and her customers. Each aspect of the process is well-defined, the Associates are well-trained, and the goals are made clear to everyone involved. We organize and staff our Financial Services, not to make it easier on us, but to provide the Jewelers with their commissions and reports in as timely a fashion as possible. And it is never organization for organization's sake, but rather organization to provide more efficient service. As the Jewelers' needs change, so does the organization.

Supervise

A well-managed company is a well-supervised company. It is important that we watch over and direct our Associates. Managers must oversee their departments and be aware of what is going on in each area. However, to supervise does not mean to boss, control, or intimidate. Supervising well ultimately means building and sustaining relationships, letting people know that they are an important part of the team, and reassuring them that their job is secure.

We do not lead by fear or intimidation at Premier Designs; we lead by caring, by serving, and by example. This doesn't mean that we don't care about job performance. We evaluate job performance on a regular basis and care enough to expect every Associate to do their very best. But caring also means that supervisors keep in close touch with their people, know how they are doing, and let them know what they do well, what can be improved, and how valuable their contribution is. We expect the best from everyone and recognize that everyone, no matter what their job is, plays a role in our success.

Direct

To direct means to "determine the course of," and at Premier this management function is crucial. We must be faithful and diligent in making sure the company stays on course, in line with our philosophy and purpose. We must keep our focus on our founding principles of Honoring God and Serving People. Management and leadership must communicate the vision of Premier consistently, and must walk it, not just talk it. We must guard against any erosion of our values and make sure that all decisions are measured against our principles, philosophy, and purpose.

When we have to make decisions, we determine our course by doing "what is right and what is best for Premier." We have repeated this phrase so often that it is now abbreviated as WIR-WBP, and everyone knows that we are referring to our basic principle for decision-making!

Appraise

Frequent appraisal of every aspect of Premier's operation is crucial. We need to know where we are and how we are doing if we are to make sure we get where we want to be. We look at our financial indicators at least weekly, and often on a daily basis. We close our month's books within a few days so we know exactly where we are financially. We stay abreast of inventory, problem jewelry, and sales trends on a daily basis so we can respond immediately. We regularly evaluate contests, promotions, paperwork, and procedures to determine what works for the Jewelers and what doesn't. We are continuously evaluating our service, training, product quality, and customer satisfaction.

Plan. Organize. Supervise. Direct. Appraise. This is the POSDA plan for managerial action, and it works.

You have heard how Joan and I started Premier and our founding vision. But Premier is not just us. It is a team of incredibly gifted people who have joined us in implementing the dream. I want you to meet some of the Team!

1989 Verse of the Year

"Work brings profit; talk brings poverty!"

PROVERBS 14:23, TLB

꙰

1990 Verse of the Year

*"Any enterprise is built by wise planning,
becomes strong through common sense,
and profits wonderfully by keeping abreast
of the facts.*

PROVERBS 24:3-4, TLB

꙰

1991 Verse of the Year

*"Seven things for us to apply:
1. Love each other.
2. Honor each other.
3. Never be lazy in our work.
4. Serve the Lord enthusiastically.
5. Be glad for all God is planning.
6. Be patient in trouble.
7. Be prayerful always."*

FROM ROMANS 12:10-11, TLB

꙰

CHAPTER TWELVE

The Marketing Team

*P*remier Designs does not belong to Joan and me. We did not build it alone. From the beginning—this has been a team effort on the part of all those in our Premier family. We could write another book telling the stories of all the people in our marketing organization who have been with us from early on and who have played important roles in building Premier. Since that's impossible, let me introduce you to some of our key couples—Premier veterans who are committed to leading Premier in the twenty-first century, building on the same philosophy, purpose, and plan that we started with.

Randy and Elizabeth Draper

Randy and Elizabeth are one of only two couples in Premier who have been appointed to the strategic position of Executive Directors. They have also achieved the Seven Diamond Designer leadership level, the highest position that can be earned in our field organization. They live with their two boys, Kyle and Kevin, in the Dallas area. Let me have Randy share in his own words their Premier story.

It was April 16, 1986, a Saturday evening. Elizabeth was shopping, and I was home working when the phone rang. A friend said, "I'm just returning the call you made to Andy earlier."

"Andy, who?" I asked, puzzled.

"Andy Horner of course."

"Well, this is funny because I never called Andy."

"Yes, you did. Yesterday afternoon you called, and I spoke with you for about ten minutes. You said you were interested in Andy's new company."

"Honestly, I didn't call. I didn't even know Andy had a new company. I thought he was still at Home Interiors."

"Andy left Home Interiors awhile ago and now he is starting his own direct sales jewelry company, Premier Designs."

Immediately I perked up. I knew Andy Horner's track record in business. At the time, Elizabeth and I had a home building business, but I was curious to hear what Andy's company involved. "I think you must have confused me with someone else. But since we're on the phone anyway, why don't you go ahead and tell me about the opportunity." She did, and I started getting excited. Of course, I knew nothing about jewelry. My wife, Elizabeth, was the kind of woman who wore only the real thing—not much of it, but the real thing. On the other hand, the ideas that were shared were exciting.

By the time Elizabeth got home from shopping, I just about attacked her at the door. "Honey, you are not going to believe this! I just learned about Andy Horner's new company. It's high fashion jewelry. You make 10 percent three levels deep and 50 percent of sales. Can you believe it! They are having a meeting tomorrow. Let's go."

Now Elizabeth was sick of me trying to push her into direct sales, but I kept trying because I knew she'd be good at it. I simply needed to find the right product. We had already tried fire extinguishers, mace, soap, water filters, cleaning materials. You name it, you could find it in our garage—a complete direct sales inventory.

"Randy, I'm not interested—period!"

"Please go," I begged.

"No! And besides, we don't have a baby-sitter."

"If I get a baby-sitter, will you go?"

"Okay," she agreed, never thinking I would find one.

I called Elizabeth's mother, who said she would baby-sit (much to Elizabeth's dismay). I spent the rest of that evening telling Elizabeth what I knew and sharing my enthusiasm. She continued to say, "That's fine. If you want to do something like that, it's your deal. I'm not interested. I don't want to get involved. Besides, the jewelry probably looks like some blue light special at K-Mart."

The next afternoon we headed out to Premier's home office for the two o'clock meeting. In the car Elizabeth took a hard look at me. "You're going to do this, aren't you? You don't care what I think. You're going to do it anyway."

"Dear, you're right. I *am* going to do it."

"I can't believe it. You don't care if I am interested or not, and I certainly am not going to do it."

"Fine," I said, "I'll do it without you."

Nothing like marital oneness. By the time we got to Premier, we weren't speaking—the perfect beginning for our new business venture!

We walked into the display room at Premier and jewelry was set out everywhere. Elizabeth began looking, and I expected the worst. Instead, a miracle happened.

"Randy, this is good looking stuff. Let's do it." I was shocked! Ten minutes before she was giving me the silent treatment—now she wanted to do this. I knew that something special had to be opening up for us.

When Andy got up to speak, I expected to hear the typical gung-ho hype about sales, the marketing plan, the product, and the "get out there and sell, recruit, and sign up as many as you can" routine. Instead, all Andy talked about was people: how we could use this business to enrich lives, how this business could meet needs in our own lives and in the lives of those we came in contact with. He talked about his vision for Premier as a direct service company, not a direct sales company. I was impressed, but was still geared into marketing. As he talked, I jotted down the names of everyone I thought might have an interest in this business. By the time he was done, I had seventy names! We signed up that afternoon and took our kit of jewelry home with us.

As it turned out, we signed up at the exact time that our home building business took a nosedive. In 1985 oil prices collapsed, and the bottom fell out of the Texas economy. This was not a good time to have eight completed spec houses ready to sell. They sat unsold for two years. During this same period, seven of the houses we were building for customers fell through. At one point we had fifteen houses sitting with For Sale signs to the tune of $28,000 to $30,000 per month out of pocket in interest alone.

I worked twelve hours a day trying to salvage our building business while Elizabeth sold Premier jewelry. I left at 7:00 in the morning, worked, and then came home for lunch and made Premier phone calls. At night I picked the kids up from the baby-sitter's and made more Premier calls, while Elizabeth was out doing home shows. Somehow, she juggled a one year old and a three year old while doing fifteen to twenty shows a month. Often she put the kids in their stroller and sold jewelry and booked home shows door to door. At the end of the day we were thrilled when we could say, "We made two hundred dollars today. Pay the electric bill."

By August of 1986, things were so bad in our construction business that we were not able to pay ourselves a thing. Amazingly, our income from Premier that month was exactly to the penny the amount we had been drawing from the building company! Looking back, Elizabeth and I believe that a guardian angel generated that first phone call from our friend. We'll be eternally grateful for how God used that to provide a way for us to pay our bills.

We worked hard to build our jewelry business, but the debts from our unsold houses kept piling up. What should we do? Was bankruptcy an option? Was there a choice? We just didn't have peace about filing. Instead, we decided to try and honor God and pay back every penny we owed. When the accountants added it all up, however the figure came to almost $750,000 with the interest accruing daily. We were desperate.

To stave off bankruptcy, we worked Premier plus a couple of other multi-level companies—anything to bring in more money. At the Premier rally in September 1987, I was out in the hallway during breaks trying to recruit Premier Jewelers into these other businesses. When Andy found out about it, he was not pleased. The following Monday he called me to his office.

He was blunt and to the point. Randy, I don't appreciate your recruiting for other businesses at a Premier function. Furthermore, as long as you chase more than one rabbit, you'll never catch any. Why don't you focus on Premier? Put your heart and soul into just one endeavor. If you will, success will come."

"Andy, you don't have any idea how much money I need to cover my debts. I need to make a million dollars this year."

He smiled. "Well, if you need to make a million dollars, then you should go into something else. But if you want to invest yourself in a business that will give you a chance to enrich lives and also give you the opportunity to make a good income, then stick with Premier. I believe that God could use Premier to pay back your debt over the next ten, fifteen, or twenty years."

I did commit to Premier full-time, and it was like God opened the floodgates of heaven. Our Premier business began to prosper in ways we could never have anticipated. After ten years, as Andy suggested, the $750,000 was paid back. We are debt-free. What an incredible witness to the power of God! The verse we held on to during this financial crisis was Jeremiah 29:11-14: "'For I know the plans I have for you,' declares the Lord, 'plans for welfare and not calamity, to give you a future and a hope... You will seek me and find me when you search for me with all your heart. I will be found by you.'"

It would be incredible enough if our story ended there. We came into Premier with a great financial burden and those needs were met. We are living proof that this works financially. But the money is not the most important thing we've received from our Premier business. The best thing has been the opportunity to build our relationship with the Lord and to be used by Him in the lives of others. God has blessed us immensely with people to work with and care about, people to share our lives and our hope with.

Our Premier experience has also provided powerful impetus for personal growth. Working together has improved our marriage. Working toward a shared goal strengthens our commitment and our communication. We have time together and more time with our boys. It has given us confidence in our worth. When we were losing all our money and going through the process of meeting with creditors, attorneys, and bankers, we felt about an inch tall. We lost our home, our cars—everything material. We felt pretty low. At such times Andy would talk about how our value was grounded in who we are as children of God, not in our financial statement. We are worth something because we are created in God's image. Our value has nothing to do with what we achieve or what we possess. We have learned to trust God when the external props have been kicked away. Premier is only beginning to teach us what it means to depend on the Lord.

Greg and Melissa Terrell

Like Randy and Elizabeth, Greg and Melissa Terrell have been appointed Executive Directors and have achieved Seven Diamond Designer status. In addition to managing their own downline, they provide wise input and helpful guidance to us at the home office. They live with their three children, Lara, Leah, and Scot, in the Houston area. Here's their Premier story.

✳

Melissa and I heard about Premier in 1987 from Randy Draper. Randy called us out of the blue to see if we might know of anyone who would be interested in Premier. A year before, Randy had contacted my brother Jack, Jr., and my parents, Beverly and Jack about signing up. Both my brother and parents had had unfulfilling experiences with direct selling companies and didn't give Randy the time of day. I guess it took him a year to get his courage back up to phone another Terrell, but looking back, we are grateful for his gumption.

Randy's call came one week after the stock market crashed in October of 1987. At the time, I was working as a stockbroker, just beginning to build up my accounts. My only income was commissions. I had been out of work for nine months prior to this job, so the crash was particularly sobering. Melissa and I were reminded again that there is no such thing as job security.

What caught Melissa's ear was Randy's statement that Elizabeth was able to stay home with their two boys, and they still made $40,000 their first year. At the time, Melissa was home with a three-and-a-half-year-old and a six-month old, doing crafts and tutoring on the side, just trying to help make ends meet. The idea of being able to stay home with the kids and still make good money was, to say the least, exciting.

I would never have talked to Randy about doing the business ourselves if he had called trying to recruit us. But he genuinely thought we wouldn't be interested. I also know we wouldn't have continued to talk to Randy about it if he hadn't mentioned that this was Andy Horner's new company. I knew the Horners from my growing-up years in Dallas. I knew that Andy Horner could be trusted. I knew he was good at what he did, and that he had integrity.

To understand the significance of what happened next, you need to know that Melissa and I are not impulsive people. We are slow, careful decision-makers and do not throw money away. Randy met with us the next day, and we signed up the following day! We asked ourselves,

"Are we crazy?" Melissa didn't even like jewelry! She had never seen a home show. Plus, my mom gently tried to steer us away, warning that people avoid you when you are in direct sales. None of that kept us from signing up. Randy was surprised. Our families were surprised. We were surprised, but we were off and running.

Melissa threw together her training show and Elizabeth came down to do it. Melissa had barely even seen the jewelry and she didn't have a clue about what she was doing. All she knew was that we needed the cash. So she gave fifteen shows in thirty-two days, completely earning back the investment we had made in the kit, and taking the pressure off financially for that month anyway. She was excited and from the first home show, loved it.

Before we got into Premier, Melissa had thoroughly enjoyed teaching school for four years. As we began our family, though, her heart was to be at home. By this time she had been a stay-at-home mom for almost four years. Many of her friends had found their own niches—things they could be involved with while mothering—but Melissa just hadn't found anything that she really loved until Premier. She enjoyed having a reason to get dressed up and be in touch with adults sometimes!

When I saw the immediate income plus what this was doing for my wife, I was sold. I thought this had to be the greatest thing any lady could consider doing. I got involved, helping to find people for Melissa to talk to about Premier. I was supportive, interested, and excited because I could see that this thing worked.

Remember, I recently had been unemployed for nine months, looking for any kind of job that would support my family. I went to dozens of places, even grocery stores, and could not get a job. It was an excruciating and humbling experience. When offered an opportunity to work with a friend in the investment business, I studied and became a broker in 1986. I was glad to have the job and worked hard at it, but it was difficult. I worked long hours and late evenings. It was slow at first, but gradually I developed some accounts and I knew that they would pan out in the long run.

The problem was that in the meantime I was having a lot more fun with Premier Designs! When I talked to people about Premier, I had more to offer them than I did as a broker. The return on their investment was so much greater, and I knew I was helping them out because it had helped us out. It gave us cash flow and gave us financial hope for the future. Finally, by April of 1989, Melissa was doing so well with Premier that we decided I should go full-time. I left the brokerage firm and happily spent my time working with my wife, building our business.

Frankly, being in business together had never been one of our goals. Before Premier we had never even thought about it. Now, we wouldn't want it any other way. Working together has given us the opportunity to be true partners. We are not only husband and wife but also business partners. We see skills and talents in one another that would never have surfaced without this Premier opportunity. Of course, it has also given us many opportunities to learn patience, understanding, and forgiveness! Premier gives us more time with our children. I am one of the few dads I know who actually does get to help raise his kids. What a privilege!

Premier has also given us the opportunity to grow spiritually. The focus of our life and business is to honor God. We don't live in one world at work and another at home. We can live our Christian lives fully throughout every activity of our day.

We never entered Premier Designs to build a business to the Four or Five Diamond level. We started so that Melissa could make a little extra income and stay at home. But from day one we loved working this business. We ended up liking it so much that it naturally evolved into a full-time business where we could work together. God brought us in contact with the right people. He grew our business. We are grateful to be part of something so wonderful—something that can truly help others.

Mike and Gayle Foster

Serving in the Atlanta area, Mike and Gayle Foster have quickly risen to the Seven Diamond Designer level. Listen to Gayle tell their story.

⚜

If you had known me before Premier I would have been the last person you would have visualized selling high fashion jewelry. I had never been to a home show of any type in my entire life. I just had no interest. As far as the jewelry was concerned, I just never thought about it, and rarely dressed up enough to wear it.

I've always loved to compete. As I grew older and married, a new interest began to stir my competitive juices. I wanted a business that my husband Mike and I could own and develop. Hardly a day went by that we didn't dream about what we could do that would enable us to work together out of our home. There wasn't anything that could be sold, or any service that could be rendered, that we didn't consider. That is, anything except direct sales and home "parties." I would have felt more confidence performing brain surgery than I would have standing up in front of a group of ladies and giving fashion tips. I just couldn't visualize myself, in this lifetime or the next, doing a home jewelry show.

During this time the unthinkable happened in my sister Janice's life. Through no choice of her own she found herself left as a single mother with two little girls to support. As God is always faithful to do, He took the heartache and confusion and through it all miraculously brought the blessing of Premier Designs into her life. As Romans 8:28 says, "God causes all things to work together for good to those who love Him, to those who are called according to His purpose."

What blew me out of the water was seeing my little sister able to totally support herself from the very first month of doing jewelry shows. I could not understand how my sister, who had never thought about any type of business, could be making more money doing home shows than I was making doing anything and everything but home shows.

Through Janice and Randy's urgings I finally "committed" with the most half-hearted commitment you have ever heard. My husband, Mike, was against it because of the questionable and manipulative techniques used by other multilevel marketing companies, and I was against it because I didn't want to ever do a home show. We came to a compromise: I would get into Premier just to get the wholesale priced jewelry, but I promised Mike I wouldn't be gone more than one night a month!

Our life changed by two events. One, we went to our first Premier rally. We could not believe what we saw. Mike saw a company that was completely different from any of the stereotypes he had formed about direct sales. At this "business rally" we were spiritually uplifted and challenged. Our hearts were stirred by stories of changed lives, of families being brought together, and of testimonies from missionaries around the world who were being supported by Premier Designs.

The second event that changed our lives was when Andy and Joan Horner came to our hometown of Memphis for a visit. Andy shared why home shows are the heart of Premier. They aren't just a good way to sell jewelry. Home shows are the best way to touch lives and spread hope. We both went away from that meeting realizing that God had indeed given us the home-based business we had wanted for so long, but with it He had also given us a vision for a ministry in others' lives who would be touched through Premier.

Four years after that date our business had grown to the point where we could devote our full-time energies to Premier. We have been able to make far more money than any other business we ever investigated. We have made lifelong friendships. Together we have been able to home school our two boys. God has used this company to give us "exceeding abundantly" more than we could have asked or thought.

༈

Three gifted families—key players on the Premier Team who have succeeded out in the field—and there are so many more. But Premier is not just the field organization. It is not just made up of people doing home shows and building their personal businesses. We also have a committed home office team of Associates and managers who service and support the Jewelers in the field.

1992 Verses of the Year

*"The person who knows right from wrong
and has good judgment and common sense
is happier than the person who is
immensely rich! For such wisdom is far
more valuable than precious jewels.
Nothing else compares with it."*

PROVERBS 3:13-15, TLB

❧

*"How much better is wisdom than gold,
and understanding than silver!"*

PROVERBS 6:16, TLB

❧

1993 Verse of the Year

"Be careful how you act."

EPHESIANS 5:15, TLB

❧

CHAPTER THIRTEEN

The Home Base Team

As Premier Designs has grown in the field, so has our home office and distribution center. We started out with six of us working, and now we have 150 Associates and managers. We are fortunate and grateful to have such a strong team of Associates, all people who really care about others and are committed to serving. I believe that God has each one at Premier for a reason.

Our management team is made up of people with a variety of skills and gifts. One remarkable thing to me is that we have never gone out looking for our managers, or used "headhunters" or other agencies to find the people we needed. Rather, as a need arose, God had the person ready and waiting. The stories of how these people got to Premier are amazing, and I wish I could tell them all. Since I can't, I'd like to have just a few of them tell you their Premier stories.

Leonard Fisher, Art Director

I received my degree from the School of the Art Institute of Chicago, specializing in graphic design and commercial art. After graduation, I returned to my home-town of Odessa, Texas, and worked as a freelance graphic artist. After eight years, my wife, Linda, and I opened an advertising agency. The agency was successful, and we opened a second office. Then the oil bust came. By 1984 we had filed for bankruptcy. We lost everything—our offices, our furnishings, our equipment. They were even about to take our house.

We decided to move to Dallas because we had family there, but we had zero money—not even enough to put gas in the truck. Some friends gave us a going-away party and gave enough cash to drive to Dallas and pay one month's rent. This was not exactly what the Art Institute had trained me for.

I began applying for jobs in the advertising industry and found myself blocked at every turn. I tried everything for five years, but nothing opened up. I even sought non-advertising jobs—like selling jewelry at department stores—and was told I was overqualified. I became discouraged and depressed.

During this period, Linda and I started a small whole-sale jewelry business, just to eat. I would make jewelry and she would sell it. It was hand to mouth, but I did learn about the jewelry business and about sales, so in retro-spect I can see how it was all working together.

In November 1990, a friend we had made through our jewelry business told us about this company called Premier Designs. When we went to her house to deliver some items, she had her jewelry set out. We loved it. In fact, Linda went nuts over it. I began looking at materials like the training manual and other printed pieces, and my response to it felt like a calling. I could see that this company needed help with their graphics. I had the training, and I believed that I was supposed to work for them.

I called Premier and spoke with the personnel manager, Ed Creek. I discovered that there was no organized graphics department and no graphics people. Ed said he didn't know if there would ever be a position but to send my resume anyway. When he received my folder of materials, he called me right away and said he would talk to Andy about me as soon as he could get him to sit down long enough, and that he would stay in touch.

In the meantime, I kept applying for other positions and was actually in line for a job at the Dallas Art Museum. I was excited about it and when I didn't hear from them for two weeks, I called to check on the status. "I'm sorry, but someone else has already been hired for that position." Evidently, my resume had gotten lost.

I was crushed. This job would have been perfect for me. But then it hit me. I knew immediately that this door had been closed because it was time to pursue a position at Premier. I stopped writing resumes and stopped applying for other positions.

In April 1991, I went to Premier and walked through the office and met some of the people. Though I still hadn't met Andy and had no position, I decided to begin working for them anyway, at home. Every morning I got up, got dressed, went to my desk, and went to work for Premier. I worked through the manual envisioning things that needed to be done. I created and revised. Linda would come home at the end of the day and ask how my day at Premier was.

After a month of this, I finally received a call from Ed and was interviewed by Andy. He offered me a two-week temporary position, which I immediately accepted. I had two weeks to produce a paper that would go out to all the Jewelers, and I didn't even know how to boot up the software programs! Somehow, it all got done and Andy was pleased.

After the two weeks were up, I just kept right on coming in to work. I was never told I had been made a permanent employee, so I figured I would keep working as a temp until they told me to leave. Well, they haven't told me to leave yet, and it has been almost ten years. It is a privilege to work here. We have come a long way in terms of our communications and graphics image, and it is gratifying to see all the pieces come together. There is a world of creative opportunities at Premier, and we have a leader who has a vision and sees the possibilities. I believe I was destined to be here. I made a lot of wrong turns, but all those turns eventually brought me to the right destination.

Jeff DiMiceli, Creative Services Manager

I vividly recall the first time my wife, Ruanne, and I attended a rally. There was so much excitement in the ballroom that weekend you could cut it with a knife. People shared hugs and laughter. Others talked about dreams and plans. Still others listened with compassion to the disappointments and hurts of friends. Me? Well, I was determined to experience everything possible. I had been to hundreds of conferences and seminars in my life. I had shared the platform with some of the best known entertainers, politicians, and religious leaders of our day. But I had never experienced anything like that Premier Designs rally. I was so captivated by the weekend that on the drive home I told Ruanne that I hoped to someday have the opportunity to help plan and produce Premier's rallies. I had no idea what was about to happen.

Most people I know would describe me as a successful church musician. For more than twenty years, I served on staff in some of the finest and largest churches in our denomination. During that time, God allowed me to lead people into areas of ministry and performance where they had never before ventured. I loved helping the average Betty and Ben develop their talents and share them with others. It amazes me how God takes average people, those who are not afraid of commitment and a little hard work, and uses them to change the world.

In many ways, Ruanne and I were the typical new Jewelers with the typical new Jeweler story. We had three growing boys who loved to eat, so she was praying for ways she could help supplement our income. Six months prior to the rally, we did not even know Premier Designs existed. Even if we had known, it would not have mattered. Several years earlier, we had hosted a direct sales "party" for another company. It turned out to be such a high-pressured fiasco, we almost lost several of our best friends. We vowed never to do it again. Trust me, a career in direct sales was not an option for Ruanne.

In April of 1991, while attending a music conference in San Diego, we bumped into a music minister from Texas who told us about his wife's jewelry business. We were mesmerized. He talked about 50 percent profit, good commissions, family time, no quotas, and lots of opportunity. Ruanne and I left that conversation knowing Premier Designs was right for us. Without ever attending a home show or seeing the jewelry, we signed up. Imagine what it was like at our house when the sample jewelry package arrived!

Ruanne's commitment and hard work paid off quickly. It was exciting to see her name in the company's newsletter and watch the number of people she sponsored grow. She reached the level of Master Jeweler, then

Designer, and then One Diamond Designer. It was fun watching her open the commission check each month. She was a card-carrying business owner. Incredible!

Meanwhile, my life was falling apart. My work situation developed problems, and my personal and spiritual priorities were completely in shambles. Before long, I reached an all-time low with no idea where to turn. It was then that I remembered hearing Andy tell about Premier Designs' affiliation with the Christian Counseling Ministry. I will be forever grateful to Joan, Andy, and Ruanne. God used their love, support, prayers, and wisdom to speak to me when I needed it most. Recovery is always a process. It takes personal determination combined with lots of support and understanding from family and friends. I was blessed with folks who cared.

After a time, I decided to call Andy and let him know I was interested in a career change. Imagine my surprise when he told me that he and Joan had been praying about developing a rally/special projects position at the home office. I could not believe what I was hearing. God was giving me the desire of my heart. Since coming to Premier Designs several years ago, I have witnessed many changes at the home office. But I am happy to say that the philosophy and purpose this company was built on is as strong as ever. Serving God and enriching lives is still paramount to everything we do.

Kenneth Hays, Procurement Services Manager

I grew up on a farm in East Texas. My grandmother told me to study and get away from the farm, so I did. After college, I went to work in the insurance industry and worked my way up.

As a hobby, whenever I went back to east Texas to visit, I bought and sold land and timber. After five years of doing that on the side, I was making more money in that business than in insurance, so I went into it full-time. I got into land, timber, oil and gas, and mineral rights, and did very well. We invested in some other businesses, and they too prospered. Things looked good. We had everything we wanted—a nice home, nice cars, country club, a nice lifestyle.

In the early eighties, I got in on the ground level of an importing and distribution opportunity that looked promising, but went sour. I tied up a great deal of my own money in the deal and lost it all. That, coupled with oil, gas, and real estate all bottoming out in the mid eighties, brought things to a head. Within five years, we were totally wiped out.

During our entire marriage, my wife Dardy had not been employed. She was able to devote herself to our marriage, our home, and our children. She enjoyed involvement in the church and community. I guess you could say that she was the typical Southern woman who was reared to let the man be the provider. For this reason I decided not to worry her about what was happening. I thought it was my problem to solve, and I wanted to protect her from it.

By the summer of 1988, however, when our home was in jeopardy, it was impossible to keep our dire situation from her. Now we had a son in law school, a daughter in college, and another son in private elementary school. Dardy had left college to marry me, so had no degree. I didn't know what she could do to help, but she wanted to do something. She immediately began substitute teaching for forty dollars a day and tutoring after school. I took jobs here and there, laying insulation in attics, whatever it took to put bread on the table. Friends and scholarships kept our kids in school.

Just before Christmas 1988, we had to move out of our beautiful home. We even had to borrow the truck to do that. Things looked grim. Lawsuits loomed against us, and friends snubbed us. We sold off most of our furniture and valuables, just to pay our bills and buy groceries.

Then that spring Dardy was invited to a Premier home show. The hostess told her that she should come and consider getting into this business. "I know the financial stress you're under, and I know you would be good at this job."

The presumption, the arrogance—Dardy wasn't about to go to this show. She hated "fake" jewelry and home "parties." Plus, she had students to tutor during the time the show was scheduled. The hostess persisted in her invitation, Dardy's students canceled, and I insisted she go check it out.

At that show, Dardy met Beverly Terrell and heard her story about being broke. She told Dardy how Premier had pulled them out of bankruptcy. A friend paid Dardy's way to Houston for a meeting where she could hear more about Premier, and she came home convinced. "I'm going to do this!" she said with conviction.

We did have one major problem, however—it cost money to get in. We had sold almost all of our things just to live. We had only one thing left—a brass and glass dining room table and chairs that Dardy loved and had hoped we could save. We sold it at an auction for three thousand dollars, bought our kit, paid our rent and utilities for the month, stocked the pantry, and went to work. We literally used our very last asset to get into the business. We knew we had no choice but to succeed.

Dardy had her training show April 20, 1989, and never looked back. We did 165 shows in the next twelve months. Dardy was number one in the nation in sales for June, July, and October, and consistently in the top five for the entire year. There was no place too far to drive. There was no time too inconvenient. We did whatever it took.

It was fascinating for me to watch—Dardy was awesome. She had never sold anything in her life, and here she was leading the company in sales! She was sponsoring people and getting good commission checks. I was impressed with the immediate cash flow, but still a little skeptical about this company that seemed too good to be true. Given the ways I had been burned by people, I think my skepticism was only natural. It didn't take long for me to be won over, though. I saw that Premier was a company that did what it said it would do. I think I was finally convinced in December 1989 when Premier overnight expressed a package to our house on Christmas Eve, so we could get it to our customer for Christmas.

In early 1990, we began to feel that God was leading us to move from Mobile to Dallas. We didn't know why we felt so strongly, but we talked about it, and I started pursuing a couple of job leads there. We knew that we would continue building her Premier business regardless of what position I found, so we decided to go ahead and move. We set August 15 as our move date, but didn't tell a soul.

By the spring of that year, a crisis was brewing at Premier. People were defecting and rumors were flying. We wondered about it, but we just kept doing what we were doing. For us, Premier was still the best show in town.

We went to Dallas in late June to find housing and make arrangements to move. It wasn't a week later that

Bruce Peterson called us in Mobile and told us that the office manager had left. He said Premier would be needing an experienced office administrator. An hour later, Andy called and asked if I would be willing to come to Dallas to the home office and help them part-time with administrative duties while still helping Dardy with her business. Of course we had already made plans to move August 15, but he didn't know that! I told him I could start on August 16.

There have been a number of transitions since August of 1990. Dardy was asked to be the National Training Coordinator and worked full-time in that position for two years. She later returned to the field, her first love, and has resumed building her business, with great success. My job has evolved from a general management position, to product manager, and now to procurement services manager. It is challenging, and a job I take very seriously. I know what Premier means to folks. I know it can mean the difference between feeding your children and not feeding your children. It made the difference for us.

James Johnson, Vice President and Assistant to the CEO

Back in 1986, I was a comptroller and corporate officer of a hardware retail chain in Houston. I had been in this position for a number of years but had decided that it would be best for me to begin looking for another opportunity. We had some friends in Dallas who knew about Andy and Premier and they told me to send a resume. I did that in January 1987 but heard nothing back. So, in February, I called Andy to ask about a possible position. He said he was headed out the door on his way to Houston to move into their new lake house on Lake

Houston. If I wanted an interview, I could come by and meet him the next morning, Saturday, and should bring my work clothes.

I did just that. I showed up on his porch in my blue jeans and helped them move. As we moved boxes and furniture, Andy and I visited. I was able to see both the burdens and the challenges he was facing as he began this new company. I immediately knew I wanted to be involved. I knew I had something to offer Premier, but more than that, I was drawn to Andy's vision of serving others and helping missions. I felt I shared his values and that we had the same heart.

Andy didn't offer me a job that day, but the more I thought about the opportunity, the more excited I got. I drove up to Dallas on Sunday and showed up at the office on Monday. I was in the lobby when Andy walked in and he was shocked. "What are you doing here?"

"I came to Dallas to get a job at Premier, and I'm not leaving until I get one. I'll do anything—fill orders in the warehouse, stuff envelopes—anything. All I know is that I'm supposed to work here!"

Well, Andy hired me. At first, I did a little of everything. Whatever needed to be done, I did it. I picked and packed, counted inventory, and answered phones. We were all a team doing whatever it took to build this company.

After eight or nine months, the company had grown to the point where my work was primarily in the accounting/financial end. Over the years, it has become even more specific, having to do with the set up and operation of the Horner-Premier Foundation, and other projects close to Andy and Joan's hearts. I am where God wants me, doing God's work at Premier, and I never plan to leave.

The Master Designer

These are just a few stories of how God put together our Premier team. If we could tell the story of every manager and every Associate, you would see how blessed we are with people who have the talents, the skills, and the experience that we need—and you would see how each of them arrived just when we needed them.

When we needed someone to head up our personnel services, the perfect man for the job lived right across the street from us: Ed Creek. As a CPA, Ed had impressive accounting and managerial experience with big eight accounting firms, but the mid eighties had been a time of personal and financial crisis. In Ed's words, "I went from the top to the bottom in six short years. I lost everything." I invited Ed and Janice to our very first Opportunity Presentation in 1985, but they had been burned by other direct sales companies so were reluctant to join us. When they decided to sign up as Jewelers in August 1989, I was delighted. Then, toward the end of that year, I realized that I needed help with personnel issues and thought of Ed. He had extensive experience and skills and a true gift of insight and caring for people. Not only has he organized and developed our Personnel Services, he also began our counseling service and prayer line for Jewelers and Associates. God had just the right man at the right time.

When we needed someone to be our distribution service manager, Lynn Hobson, a godly young man with warehouse experience, was looking for just such a job. Kevin Moses, a young man with strong people skills and a caring heart, whose wife was a Jeweler, felt led to come help us at Premier. He began by overseeing our Jeweler and Customer Services department and is now our Marketing Administration Manager.

When I was first thinking of writing up the story of Premier, my daughter Andrea was ready for a career change and available to come to Dallas. Not only did she spend much time researching and writing, but she also has assumed the position of Special Projects Services Manager and produces and organizes our rallies and special events. Joan and I had been planning and coordinating all those events, but it was getting to be too big a job for us. God knew our need and met it.

At exactly the time our accounting and financial services needed to be expanded and updated, God had just the man. Elbert Johnson, an able and skilled young man whose wife was a Jeweler, was available to come. Several more gifted people have become part of our management team: Don Cook as Director of Operations Services, A. B. Taylor as Training Director, Linda Stefanides as Customer Services Manager, Becky Williams as Director of Customer Services and Quality, and Kevin Melton as Office Services Manager.

A few years ago we introduced a prayer ministry program headed by Beverly Draper. We have hundreds of requests each month. It is a service greatly appreciated by our Premier family. We are so blessed with a management team that believes in Premier and our philosophy and ministry.

Joan and I could not—and did not—do this alone. I believe we have the best home office team of any direct sales company in America, because every member of our team has been brought to Premier by the Master Designer—at exactly the right time and with something specific to contribute. There are no accidents. This is not the luck of the Irish. This is by design.

PART THREE

The Proof of Premier

1994 Verse of the Year

*"For our people must learn to help all who
need their assistance, that their lives
will be fruitful.*

Titus 3:14, TLB

❧

1995 Verse of the Year

*"Commit to the Lord whatever you do,
and your plans will succeed.*

Proverbs 16:3, NIV

❧

1996 Verse of the Year

*"And all the people were very happy
because of what God had accomplished
so quickly."*

2 Chronicles 29:36, TLB

❧

CHAPTER FOURTEEN

The Purpose Realized

I'm sure that by now you have gotten our message: The purpose of Premier is *To Enrich Every Life We Touch*. We want to enrich the lives of those who join our Premier family, and we want them to catch the vision of enriching the lives of those they come in contact with—their hostesses, customers, and each other. Most people join us for the money. They have financial needs and this is their primary motivation at the outset. We want them to meet these needs. We designed a good payout on sales and a generous commission structure for that very reason. But there is more—and that "more" is serving others, caring, and sharing.

Does it work? Are people's lives better because of Premier? Have our Jewelers caught the vision? Are they motivated beyond the money to serve others? The proof of the pudding is in the eating, and Joan and I have the privilege of hearing from so many about all that is happening in their lives. We could fill volumes with their Premier stories. Why don't you look over our shoulders for a few minutes and read a sampling of excerpts from the many letters we have received, so you can see for yourselves the proof of Premier.

Jewelers' Lives Enriched by Personal Growth

Dear Andy and Joan,

When I joined Premier, I thought I would be selling jewelry to earn a little extra income. I had no idea how this company would help to change my life! Premier has given me the courage to be the outgoing, positive person that God intended me to be. My confidence has grown as I've stood in front of ladies at home shows. I now take better care of myself and take more pride in my personal appearance. The financial rewards have been wonderful, but nothing compared with the emotional gains.

—Rosemary Berry of Roswell, Georgia

Dearest Andy and Joan,

I thank God that He gave you a vision for Premier and that you obeyed His call. Premier has opened up a whole new world for me. I was a stay-at-home mom, a priority for my husband and me, with very few friends and extremely low self-esteem. After four years with Premier, the wonderful people, spirit, and leadership, I found that I could learn and do something that made me feel good about me. It built my confidence in myself, which I never had, and I began to like myself.

—Sharon Summers of Brandon, Mississippi

Jewelers' Lives Enriched by Being Part of the Premier Family

Dear Andy and Joan,

You cannot imagine how you have touched my life. I look back at the past three and a half years and am amazed by what has happened in my life. My first year in Premier

I didn't do much because of my Air Force job. I finally got going in February 1992 and was in full swing that summer, when hurricane Andrew came and wiped out all my material possessions. I will never forget the kindnesses that you and others in Premier showed me. You, the folks in the home office, and my Premier family were all there for me. It was amazing the love and support I received. You all kept encouraging me and telling me that God was with me. I had no money. I had no material possessions. But I had never felt so much love and peace.

—Ann Edlund of Summerville, South Carolina

Dear Joan and Andy,

I joined "the Premier Family" in January 1991. It was something I never dreamed of doing and it has made such a difference in my life. I am an only child and have lost my mom and dad. I have my husband and our four sons, but they are all grown. Premier has given me a new family that means so much to me. I love everyone in my Premier family and there is not a thing I wouldn't do for them. I have made friends I would never have made if it had not been for Premier. It has given me people to love and who love me, and something to do that I really enjoy. For this, I thank you very much.

—Johnalee Gray of Memphis, Tennessee

Jewelers' Lives Enriched by Spiritual Growth

To Our Dearest Friends Joan and Andy:

Where do we start in telling you what you and Premier have meant to Kay and me? Not only have you given us an opportunity to grow a profitable business and push our God-given talents to their limits, but, most importantly,

you have guided us spiritually. Beyond a shadow of a doubt, the best thing that has come of our years with you and Premier has been our faith in God. We had gotten a little off track, but now our faith grows stronger each day.
—Jim and Kay Robinson of Marietta, Georgia

Dear Joan and Andy,
Our family has benefited in so many ways from our involvement in Premier. We've certainly benefited monetarily, but more than that, we have grown in our relationship with the Lord, and that is a direct result of being associated with the Premier family. Thank you for that.
—Nancy Dearman of Clinton, Mississippi

An Unexpected Blessing: Marriages Enriched and Families Strengthened

One of the joys of Premier for Joan and me has been to see so many couples doing this business together and seeing many families strengthened. Some husbands do home shows while others support their wives by caring for the children. It has become a joint venture for many couples. When we see hundreds of husbands at our rallies, it warms our hearts. We didn't plan it that way. I wouldn't have known how to do it. It is something the Lord has done—a totally unexpected blessing.

Dear Joan and Andy,
Premier came into our lives before our marriage did. In fact, our entire married life is a direct result of Premier. My wife was selling Premier jewelry to put herself through college. She sponsored me into Premier so I could pay off some debt so I could marry her. We thought I would be

an engineer and she would be a dietitian and that Premier would just last through college. Little did we know!

We attended a meeting in Memphis that changed our life direction. You spoke, but you did not talk hype or money. You talked about serving people and making a difference in America. Michelle and I knew that this was what we wanted to do—and that we wanted to do it together. Our lives will never be the same. We are working together in a business we love, impacting lives, and making a difference. Because of your vision, we are living our dream.

—Keith and Michelle Gray of Nashville, Tennessee

Dear Joan and Andy,

It is difficult to put into words what Premier has meant to us. The Lord has used Premier to provide for our family, to draw us closer together, and to allow us more time to raise our own children. It has given us opportunities to minister to our hostesses and to our Premier family, and has given us the best friends we have ever had! Thanks, Joan and Andy!

—Don and Tandy Flynn of Lexington, Kentucky

Jewelers' Enriching the Lives of Others

Dear Joan and Andy,

We are so excited to be associated with Premier. We are grateful to you for proving to the business community that a company can be successful that honors God and loves and serves people. We are so grateful for the lives you have touched and for the opportunity Premier has given us to be involved in loving and serving others. And to think that we joined Premier just to add a little money to our retirement checks!

—Marge and Chuck Caldwell of Houston, Texas

Dear Joan and Andy,

Premier came to us in November of 1989, one year before I got laid off. Little did we know how much we would need Premier financially and spiritually that next year. I have seen my wife Lisa's confidence grow and our love for each other grows stronger each year. Premier has been a constant source of strength and inspiration to us. We look forward to our years ahead with Premier. To be involved in a business with Premier's philosophy and purpose, that offers us an opportunity to impact so many lives, is truly a miracle.

—Less and Lisa Kilday of Houston, Texas

Dear Joan and Andy,

Premier is a miracle company that has truly honored God and served thousands of people. We would never have thought, or imagined, that such a company could exist in secular America. Premier may be the only business in America that provides an opportunity for spiritual growth and encourages ministering to others above money. Outside our church ministry, we are more excited about Premier than anything we have ever been involved in.

—Fred and Leigh Lowery of Bossier City, Louisiana

Dear Joan and Andy,

We feel very blessed to be a part of Premier. Every day our Premier business brings us opportunities to serve and minister to others in ways we never before thought possible. Premier has allowed us to leave the stressful, demanding corporate world and have time to give to our children and grandchildren, as well as time to be with each other. The personal growth and rewards we receive through Premier continue to amaze us. Working with the people we sponsor and seeing them grow and meet their needs through their Premier businesses is a joy that enriches our lives.

—Larry and Bernice Parker of Myrtle Beach, South Carolina

1997 Verse of the Year

"The LORD says, "I will guide you along the best pathway for your life. I will advise you and watch over you."

PSALM 32:8, NLT

❧

1998 Verse of the Year

"For I know the plans I have for you," *declares the LORD, "plans to prosper you and not to harm you, plans to give you hope and a future."*

JEREMIAH 29:11, NIV

❧

CHAPTER FIFTEEN

Dreams Fulfilled

When Joan and I started Premier, we dreamed of a company that would give mothers the opportunity to be home with their children, that would provide a way for single mothers to support their families and still be with their kids, that would allow ministers' wives to supplement the family income and find an identity of their own, and that would support missionary endeavors both here and around the world. These dreams have been fulfilled in ways that we could not have imagined back in 1985. Read what these Jewelers have to say.

Moms Get to Stay Home

Dear Andy and Joan,

It is just amazing how the Lord continues to bless you and His work through you. Our boys have become so excited about Premier and the opportunity it has provided for Pauline to be at home with them every day. Premier is such an integral part of our lives and family that we just want to say thank you for your vision for Premier and your steadfastness in seeing it through.

—Pauline and Kent Meier of Centreville, Virginia

Dear Andy and Joan,

I am so thankful God put Premier in my life. I was recently offered the full-time position of fashion coordinator for a clothing store chain. I had previously enjoyed this line of work and have several years of experience. If I took the job, it would mean that my three-year-old and nine-month-old would have to start going to daycare, but even so it was appealing. But after the Premier rally in Atlanta, I knew what my decision would be and I knew I was doing the right thing. I can do home shows four to eight nights a month for my business and make the same money I could working twenty or more days each month for someone else's business—and I can be home with our children. Premier has so much to offer and it sure came through for me. Thank you.

—Lynda and Jeff Soss of Savannah, Georgia

Single Moms Can Support Their Kids

Dear Andy and Joan,

A little over twelve years ago, I joined Premier. Recently married, I saw Premier as an opportunity to help buy the extras we couldn't afford. At that time, we worked with college students at a small Christian school. Later I realized the long term potential and options I would have if I continued to build my business. My heart's desire was not to put my child in daycare when I had a child. After ten years of marriage, Premier had become our full-time income and my daughter was born. Little did I know that three years later I would become a single mom. I know God has used Premier to provide for Lacy and me financially. In addition, Premier has been a source of friend-

ships, support, growth, and hope that I can share with others. Thank you for letting me be a part of the dream!
—Dana Reid of Charlotte, North Carolina

Dear Andy and Joan,

Like most people, I got in this business to earn extra income. As a single parent and sole support of my four-year-old son, Taylor, I had to do something since my secretarial salary just didn't cut it. Little did I know how much I would gain—an extended family, lifelong friends, a strengthening of faith and persistence, and learning to love and accept people even if they don't always do what they say they will! It is out of financial, emotional, and spiritual necessity that I continue this business. In the words of my now eleven-year-old son, "Our lives wouldn't be the same without Premier."
—Paula Crockett of Spring, Texas

Dear Andy and Joan,

A couple of years ago, when I was on the verge of finalizing a painful divorce after fourteen years of marriage, I was struggling financially as well as emotionally. Little did I know that through Premier my life would be changed forever. A prudent businessperson would gauge the benefits of Premier by the "bottom line"—and that has been well above my wildest expectations. But that is just the tip of the iceberg in terms of what Premier has done for me as a single mom. The biggest treasures to come from my association with Premier have been friendships, the reaffirmation of values, and hope—something I had not felt for a long time. Now, not only have I been able to re-establish myself, but I recently purchased a beautiful home in my own name! From the bottom of my heart, thank you,

Andy and Joan, for taking the time to give your attention and love to those who need it most—single moms like me!
—Pamela Bollinger of Milford, Ohio

Helps Those in Full Time Ministry

Dear Andy and Joan,

My Premier story started in a very tragic way four years ago when our fifteen-year-old daughter ran away from home. Up to that point, I had had a perfect, storybook life. All of a sudden, my daughter was gone and I didn't know where she was. My marriage began falling apart. My husband is the pastor of a large church and because our marriage was troubled, things at the church began to go wrong. In just a few short weeks, my wonderful storybook life was totally wrecked. I became depressed, even suicidal.

About seven or eight months later, I was introduced to Premier and signed a contract, without ever having been to a home show. I was looking for a little job, a way to make an extra fifty to one hundred dollars a week, but hadn't worked in twenty years. I had no idea what was in store for me!

God used Premier to help me with my emotional healing. My only identity up to that point had been to be the pastor's wife and the mother of four children. I had no other identity. I didn't even know anyone outside of our church. Premier opened up a whole new world to me. It gave me confidence and purpose. I have met over one thousand ladies that I never would have met, and have seen God work through me in serving them.

My daughters are now in college and our Premier money is helping pay for that. My family has been put back together. My marriage has been restored. Our church is

moving ahead once again. I thank God for Joan and Andy Horner and for Premier and what it has meant in my life.
—Linda Masteller of Oklahoma City, Oklahoma

Dear Andy and Joan,

At the time Premier was introduced to me, I was teaching first grade, assisting my husband, Dick, in his church music ministry, and trying to meet the needs of our two daughters. We knew that our girls needed more of my time and attention, but there wasn't more time I could give them. Though our church was providing a solid living, we had financial needs beyond one salary. Financially, we were barely making it. We recognized that we needed to make a change for our daughters' sakes.

Dear friends of ours invited us to dinner to share a business opportunity. I really didn't absorb the details of the business, but I could see the genuine joy and excitement in their faces. It was obvious that this had affected their lives for good.

Dick immediately knew that this was for us. For the first time, he saw hope for our financial future. It sounded good, but I knew that I could not possibly stand in front of a group of ladies and sell jewelry! The struggle over personally committing to this business went on for months. I would tell our friend yes, and then fear and self-doubt would reign, and I would back out. This inner conflict went on for months. Finally, school was ending, and I decided to step out in faith and trust God. He was faithful in dealing with my overwhelming fear. I still remember driving to home shows and feeling so frightened that tears would run down my cheeks. God enabled me to do what seemed impossible.

Then, something began to happen. I met ladies who were delighted I was there. They loved the jewelry and the fashion tips. I loved doing home shows. I loved the jewelry. I loved the new friends I was making and the confidence I felt. My friends at church noticed a difference in me. I was changing.

I have always loved Dick's music ministry, and I have always cherished being his wife, but at times my identity seemed lost as an individual. God used Premier in my life to help me understand that I was special to Him as a person. He has given me a personal ministry to ladies outside of our church that I could never touch any other way.

God blessed us financially, which gave Dick more freedom in his ministry. Premier allowed me to give our girls the time they needed, and now it is allowing us to send them through college. A few years ago we could not imagine how we were going to be able to pay for that!

Dick and I look at our lives and cannot imagine life without Premier. We have grown personally, spiritually, and financially. We thank God for you both and for Premier. It is so much more than just a jewelry company. —Dot Hill of Houston, Texas.

Supports Missions Around the World

Joan and I have always been involved in missions in America and other countries. It was because of our desire to support ministries that we were motivated to launch Premier. Our prayer was that the company would be used to provide security and income to all who joined us and that there would be overflow to send to ministries at home and abroad.

Supporting missions is not something that we market or use to persuade people to join Premier. It is a private endeavor that we are privileged to be a part of. Here are excerpts from a few of the many letters we receive each month letting us know how God is working around the world.

Dear Andy and Joan,

God is doing incredible things here in Venezuela. In the past ten months, 1,322 decisions for Christ have been made and 1,308 dedications. We had an exciting five weeks of summer camp where many people gave their lives to Christ. Next year, we will start a training program called MED (Ministry, Evangelism, and Discipleship). Pray with us that this program will enable laypersons to go back in their community to serve God more effectively.

God has provided for the construction of a medical clinic in the jungle. This clinic and the many conferences held there will reach many for Christ. We thank God for the prayers and support of Premier Designs people who believe in the importance of reaching others for Christ.
—Alvaro Ripoli, Caracas, Venezuela

Dear Premier Family,

Greetings from the "Land of Smiles." Thank you for your letter of encouragement and interest in our ministry. There are many who aren't really interested in what takes place here. Your letter was timely and encouraged us. On behalf of my husband and children, we thank you and love you for your love for Jesus and your desire to see unsaved people passed from death unto life. Because of your help and love, we can continue being missionaries here, where our home and our hearts are.
—Kathy Omer, Bangkok, Thailand

Dear Premier Family,

Our hearts are full of joy for what the Lord has done during this summer at our camps. We had 400 campers.

Thirty-one came to know the Lord as Savior and 236 dedicated their lives to serve Him. Thank you so much for your continued help in prayer and in support.
—The Portillos, Pergugia, Italy

Dear Friends,
So much has happened this spring. Evangelism in schools resulted in over 450 being saved. Evangelism in churches resulted in about 300 being saved. EuroYouth was a wonderful success with 97 young people responding for world missions. Thanks so much for your faithfulness in prayer and in finances.
—Eric Murphy, Budapest, Hungary

Dear Brothers
Greetings from Mexico City. We are very busy these days in preparations for our Summer Camp. We hope to have over 120 children and trust in the Lord that we will see many miracles of salvation. Please be praying for us in this special time of ministry. I am including with this letter a picture of our staff with the minivan that we received from you. We as staff appreciate that gift so much. May God bless you according to His riches.
—Leonardo DiGilio, Mexico City, Mexico

Dear Friends,
I want to take this opportunity to express our deepest gratitude to you for your continued monthly support and donating Christmas presents to the children of the Matamoros Baptist Children's Home. Please continue lifting us up in your daily prayers.
—Dr. & Mrs. Saul Camacho, Matamoros, Mexico

Dear Premier,
With much joy and happiness in my heart I have received your letter. I want to sincerely thank you for your

practical support that I receive each month from you. Thank you for being part of our ministry here in Chile. It is my desire that the Lord blesses you richly.

—Jorge Daut, Santiago, Chile

Dear Premier friends,

We always praise God for Andy and Joan's vision to support God's work around the world. They have been of much encouragement during these past years to all of us who are serving the Lord with Word of Life in Latin America. What a beautiful thing it is to belong to the same team for the cause of Jesus Christ!

—Ruben y Graciela Matos, Lima, Peru

Dear Andy and Joan,

I just want you to know how grateful I am from the depths of my heart for your consistent service to me and to our ministry. Thank you for your generous gifts to CitiVision, Transformation Life Center, the Love Kitchen, and the Manhattan Bible Church. Thousands of people are being blessed and are encouraged daily because of your generosity. Thank you.

—Tom and Vicky Mahairas, New York City, New York

Dear Premier Friends,

We are grateful for your good letter and want to thank you for the encouragement it is for us to know that you are upholding us in prayer. It is really wonderful to see all the exciting things that God is doing through Ireland Outreach. We thank you for being partners with us in this ministry. We are truly humbled and continue to praise the Lord for the privilege of being His servants.

—Jim and Jean Gillette, Dublin, Ireland

Dear Brethren,

I wish to write to you with my own hands to thank you very much for your gifts and prayers. You have a part in our lives and ministry in Colombia; our fruits in the Lord are your fruits too. We love you and thank you, beautiful friends.

—Manuel Gomez, Colombia, South America

Dear Friends at Premier,

I would like to express my appreciation for your gift. Thank you for participating in our ministry in this way. Many things are happening here in Poland. During the first four weeks of our camping season, 315 people made salvation decisions and 160 made dedication decisions! We thank God and thank you for your interest in our ministry. Thank you for your desire to pray for us. Your prayers mean very much to us.

—Maly and Ewa Dwulat, Warsaw, Poland

Dear Brothers in Christ,

God blessed us with a great summer camp season. Thank you very much for your love, faithful prayers, and support. You are a part of our ministry here in Argentina.

—Andres Fernandez Paz and Dan Nuesch, Buenos Aires, Argentina

Jewelers' Dreams Fulfilled

Not only have Joan's and my dreams been fulfilled, so have the dreams of many of our Jewelers. For example, Sandra Peters has a son named Justin, who was diagnosed with cerebral palsy when he was eleven months old. Because of his special needs, she needed work that allowed her to be with him in the morning until he left and when he got home in the afternoon. She was a teacher's assistant for many years—until she heard about Premier. She realized she could make more money in less time and be available to take care of Justin.

Sandra and her husband did everything they could to encourage Justin's independence and self-sufficiency. Once he reached high school, having his own transportation was a major aspect of that self-sufficiency. Because he got around in a motorized scooter, he needed a van with a lift, quite an expensive purchase. Sandra decided that she would do extra home shows just for Justin's van and save the money they needed to buy it.

Well, Justin got that van in time for his senior year of high school! Now, he is driving it to college. Premier money has helped pay his college tuition for the past four years, and now his younger sister's as well. Sandra said, "Premier has met our financial needs, and more. I have a real difficult time trying to express just how I feel about Premier and what it has done for us."

James and Cherri Karr had a different kind of dream. Here's what they wrote:

Dear Andy and Joan,

A lot of changes have taken place in the past seven years. In 1987, my husband, James, felt the desire to build a house for our family—with his own hands! Since James works for the state park service, we have always gotten our housing from the state. Just as he started on our house (working every day off), we found that we were expecting a new baby. I needed to be at home for the baby, but I also needed to help send our two older children through college and help buy materials for our house. The Lord allowed us to become a part of a wonderful company, Premier Designs, which helped meet all those needs.

This is the seventh year since these things began, our year of JUBILATION! Our house is finished, our "baby" is going into first grade, our older children are out of college, raising children of their own, and I have been able to be home with my family and still have a growing business!
—Cherri Karr of Whitney, Texas

1999 Verse of the Year

"There is a time for everything, a season for
every activity under heaven.
A time to be born and a time to die.
A time to plant and a time to harvest."

Ecclesiastes 3:1-2, nlt

※

2000 Verse of the Year

"But they that wait upon the LORD shall
renew their strength; they shall mount up
with wings as eagles; they shall run, and
not be weary; they shall walk,
and not faint."

Isaiah 40:31, kjv

※

Conclusion

I'm Michael. Remember me from the beginning of the book? I'm Linda's husband who promised to share with you why Premier has changed our lives. I'm sitting here in this gigantic Dallas Convention Center surrounded by thousands of women and a lot of their husbands. As Andy's "Lest We Forget" speech charges towards its conclusion, I'm thinking, *Why are there tears on my cheeks?*

I'm a baby boomer. I've lived through the *Forrest Gump* years and they were not a box of chocolates. For me, life's been more like a box of firecrackers that keep blowing up in my face. I saw my teammates go from sweating it out at a high school football game on a Friday night to being blown apart by booby traps in the steamy jungles of Viet Nam. But soon, the Peter, Paul and Mary flower children, who sang about love and caring for one another, took off their torn jeans and cut their braids. Then, decked in their new Armani suits and at the wheels of their Mercedes, they pushed to take over Wall Street, pushing after the almighty dollar just like their parents of the fifties.

The sixties, seventies, and eighties infected my heart with a hopeless, cynical despair. My slogans became: "Everyone's got an angle," "Don't trust a soul over thirty," and "You can't believe in anyone or anything!" The image of Andy Horner, this Irish kid turned American, flashes before me on the big screen. I can also look to the front of this auditorium and see the real man, humbly sitting on a stool sharing his heart—the wisdom of over seventy years of life experience.

Maybe my cheeks are wet with tears because "The Star Spangled Banner" really does mean something. There actually were flesh and blood Americans who believed enough in freedom, free enterprise, and the right of the individual to pursue life, liberty, and happiness to shed their blood. Maybe there is something to letting others know that you love and appreciate them. What else could cause women to light up like the sun when they are applauded and recognized for their faithfulness, not just their sales, before thousands of their peers? Maybe words like honesty, integrity, faith, responsibility, and caring still do have meaning and provide a true foundation that makes even a simple transaction, like purchasing some jewelry, more than just dollars and cents?

And all this talk about God, Jesus Christ, and the Bible—perhaps it's time for me to stop reacting to the way my parents crammed religion down my throat and stop using the worn out college sophomore rebuttal against faith: "Look at all the hypocrisy in the lives of those who profess it." After all, if this whole spiritual thing is bogus, why do I get so angry at a TV evangelist who is immoral? Maybe it's because deep inside, I do know what the real Jesus Christ stands for and who He actually is. I'm thinking I might sit down with Andy, or one of the other leaders of Premier, and have a talk about their personal Jesus thing.

Premier isn't for everyone. Not everyone is going to travel around their town or city doing home shows. If they did, who could be invited to buy the jewelry? But everyone needs to take a long, thoughtful look at the values that Premier stands for. As we move into the twenty-first century, you might even find more to get excited about than Bill Gates's latest offering from Microsoft. (I know I shouldn't let my mind wander while someone else is talking.) I just caught Andy Horner saying something about purpose. He usually gets the last word in Premier, so it's only fitting to listen in as he drives home his message:

The purpose of Premier, *our* purpose, is to enrich every life we touch. We believe in a God who is able to help us to do this. Our plan is to go into the homes of America and bring hope where there is often divorce, despair, and meaninglessness. We want to help people smile again. Does this mean everyone is going to love you? Does this mean you will all be tremendously successful? Does this mean it will be easy? No!

When I was in the Baylor heart unit a few years ago, God was good to me. He gave me a warning signal before I self-destructed. I remember lying there in surgery looking at the video of my heart as the doctors maneuvered their scope and their "rotor rooter" to clean out my arteries. While they worked on my heart, I said to the doctor, "Where are the batteries for that thing?" He said, "What thing?" "My heart. What keeps it beating? Where do you have it plugged in?" He laughed and kept probing. "I guess it's just a little luck," he said. "No way!" I said. "It's not by chance. It's an answer to prayer. Don't you realize you have an army of my family and friends praying for your skillful hands right now, many of them right out there in the hallway?"

The cardiologist finished his delicate vascular plumbing job, and they rolled me into intensive care. Lying in the bed next to mine was a man whose stomach was all cut up from a fight the night before. Across from me was a lady who was not expected to live. I couldn't move, but then a quiet peace came over me. Never in my life have I had such a peace! Never so much joy! Folks, when I came out of that hospital, I came out with a message—a message I'm going to proclaim regardless of what anyone says.

I believe there is a God who created us in His image. Made "in the image of God" means that every one of you is priceless and needs to be treated with tenderness and respect.

I believe in my mom's tattered old Bible and the biblical principles she taught me from the beginning way back in Belfast. I spent years rebelling against the Bible; then years defending it; now, I just let it speak for itself. It can fight for itself. It will endure.

I believe in the Bible's message—the power of Jesus Christ to give us forgiveness and eternal life. His personal presence in my life is my hope and joy.

I believe in the power of practicing the truth, not just preaching it. There have been enough high sounding sermons. What people need to see are the actions. At Premier we want to live what we say. We need the actions of commitment to home, to church, and to our country. The home should be more than a place of wood, bricks, and furniture. It should be a place where a family can find love, true values, and acceptance. Without my faithful, skilled wife at my side, there would be no Premier. There would be no fulfillment of our dreams. She's not just my lover. She's my best friend.

Is Premier a Christian company? No! There's no such thing as a "saved company." Jesus died and rose again for individuals, not for corporations. Do you have to be a Christian to become a part of our company? Absolutely not! We are going to love and accept you, right where you are, and whatever you believe. I do believe in the Bible and in Jesus Christ. I believe in Him because I have actually seen His power change my life, and Joan's life, and thousands of others. But every individual has to decide for himself or herself. Does this commitment to honoring God mean that we don't do our homework when it comes to business procedures and accounting practices? Look at the books and our operating procedures for yourself. You've seen the graphs and tables of our solid, controlled growth. The label "Christian" never becomes an excuse for sloppy business in this company.

It's the American Dream—to arrive in North America as an immigrant, the son of an alcoholic father and a scrub lady, and to rise to the top of a multi-million dollar company. I've lived this dream, but the real riches come only when you learn to focus your life on enriching others. It's when you start giving yourself away that your real bank account begins to swell. Premier's bank account is full. We are financially strong. But the true wealth is sitting right here before me. It's *you*, and all those who have united with us to honor God and to enrich every life we touch, as we bring a dose of hope into homes across America. All this didn't happen just by chance. The Ultimate Designer brought this about and He will see it to the end.

2001 Verse of the Year

"Give thanks to the Lord and proclaim
His greatness, let the whole world know
what He has done."

PSALM 105:1 NLT

✵

2002 Verse of the Year

"Let your light shine before men,
that they may see your good works
and glorify your Father who is in heaven."

MATTHEW 5:16 NLT

✵

2003 Verse of the Year

"Choose a good reputation over great riches, for
being held in high esteem is better than having silver
or gold."

PROVERBS 22:1 NLT

✵

Appendix:
A Time Line

1924   Born in Belfast, Ireland

1931   My mother decides to emigrate to America, leaving Belfast, Charleville Street, friends, and the land she loved. Due to health reasons, we are redirected to Woodstock, Ontario, Canada.

1932   Plan to attend the Brethren Assembly, but are not received because of no letter of commendation. End up at Oxford Street Baptist Church.

1934   School district lines change. Live on north side of street and transfer to Princess School. In school with Joan Taylor all through high school.

1935   Accept Jesus Christ as my Savior at Oxford Street Baptist Church.

1940   Mother purchases a Ford car for me to drive her to the building we are cleaning at night. This car is my ticket into the Joan Taylor group—a step up for an "East Ender" in Woodstock.

1941   Joan is secretary to Lee Forbes, formerly of Austin, Texas.

1943   Join the Royal Canadian Navy at seventeen and a half years of age to get away from home and serve my country.

1945   Home on leave and date Joan Taylor. Discharged in October, and I am much in love.

1946   Marry Joan March 9. This is unthinkable as we are from different economic and social class backgrounds.

1949   Because of Joan's desire to live in America, we apply for our visas.

1950   Board a train and enter America through Buffalo. Head to Boston area to work for my brother. This does not work out, so we head for Austin, Texas. Eight weeks later, I find a temporary job at seventy-five cents per hour with Texas Highway Department. Go to work Monday morning. The place is empty as it is May 30—Memorial Day. We make a hasty decision to go to Dallas, Texas, where we know no one. Dallas has never been in our thoughts or discussions. We make contact with Bill and Mary Blair. Bill has a brother, Bert, in Woodstock who told us to look him up. Joan finds a job at Reserve Life. Works for a Christian supervisor, Marie Hunter.

1951   Invited to church by one of Joan's associates, Mrs. Ritchie. End up at First Baptist of Dallas. April 29, Joan accepts Jesus as her Savior, and I rededicate my life to God. One of the first people we meet is Mary Crowley. She is Joan's Sunday school teacher.

1952   At Texas Unemployment Commission, I overhear information about an opening for a supervisor at Johnson Wax. Land job despite no college degree.

1960   Promoted at Johnson Wax and relocate family to Racine, Wisconsin. Meet Don and Marion Placko, our apartment neighbors.

1961   Plackos introduce us to Word of Life ministries.

1963   Return to Dallas and join Xerox Corporation.

1967   Accept a transfer and plan a move to California. Have a check in my spirit and remain in Dallas.

1968   Get reacquainted with Mary Crowley, who founded Home Interiors and Gifts. In July, I accept a position at Home Interiors.

1972-1974   We meet with Bruce and Maggie Peterson at Word of Life in Schroon Lake, New York.

1982   On a trip to Israel, Bruce Peterson introduces us to Bob and Anne Moore.

1984   I leave Home Interiors and resolve never to get involved in direct sales again. Bob Moore calls several times and invites us to Argentina.

1985   In January we make our first trip to Argentina and Uruguay—our first exposure to national missions. In February we receive a call from CPA and friend, Wendell Judd, which results in consulting with a direct sales jewelry company. Opportunity to get the company for practically nothing. I am excited, but my lawyer refuses to approve or let me accept the company. In August we travel to Poland, behind the Iron Curtain, with Dave Wyrtzen. This gives me plenty of time to share my heart. Dave's counsel is to use my talents as an entrepreneur. Howard and Hazel Goddard stop by unexpectedly in October and encourage us to "go for it." Found Premier Designs on November 5 and establish the philosophy, purpose, and plan.

1990   Company splits when the president at the time starts his own business. Formation of the Premier Prayer Partner Association.

1995   Premier Designs' tenth anniversary. Business retails over 60 million dollars, with 6,000 leaders and Jewelers.

1996   Remodel Haven of Hope Training Center.

1997   Reorganize management, adding General Manager and Quality Control Manager positions.

1998   Establish Training Director position. Pay off home office building mortgage. Establish website. Joan Horner promoted to Executive Vice President.

1999   Break ground for addition to Premier Designs home office.

2000   Celebrate Premier Designs' fifteenth anniversary with a national rally in the Dallas Convention Center. The Premier family is joined by many of our prayer partners and missionaries from America and around the world.

2001   Move-in completed for newly constructed reception center at Home Office. Construction begins on new distribution center and warehouse at Home Office. Active Jeweler base tops 10,000.

2002   New distribution center and warehouse opens at Home Office.

2003   Steady continued growth throughout the year.

An Irish Creed

"Will is something to treasure;

Charm is something to love;

Peace is something to keep;

Love is something to give;

Joy is something to find;

God is the One to thank

From now to the end of time."

AUTHOR UNKNOWN

✤